*"In my work with tens of thousan_____
nation, I've found that great teachin_____*
on WHAT I'm going to teach or HOW I'm going to teach it.
Extraordinary moments in the classroom are always based on
WHY I'm teaching. With a big enough WHY, the WHAT and
the HOW always seem to fall into place. Read **The Power of a
Teacher** and allow it to rekindle the why in your heart— both
you and your students deserve it."*

—Hal Bowman
Twenty-year Teaching Veteran and
Author of *TEACH LIKE A ROCK STAR*

"Adam is indeed a rare breed of psychologist: a refreshing—
even uncanny—ability to merge science with practice, and
a teaching style that's not only insightful, but actually fun.
If you're looking for a tool to build health and unity on your
campus, you just found it."

—Chris White, Ph.D.,
Director of Research, The Flippen Group
Co-author of New York Times Best Selling *THE FLIP SIDE*

*"Beginning with his own inspiring story, Adam has
masterfully collected poignant narratives capturing the power
of teachers to change lives in profound and lasting ways. But
Adam knows mere stories are not enough to transform practice.
Perspective, insight, and wisdom from these stories must be
garnered and shared to harness the power needed for meaningful
transformation. **The Power of a Teacher** will warm hearts, but
more importantly, it will illuminate and inform practice."*

—Trae Kendrick, Ed.D.
Former Teacher, Principal, and Current State-level
Educational Leader

"The message you are sharing is a powerful one that many people need to hear over and over again."

J.D., Teacher, Bryan Independent School District

"Your ideas are great, and I can't wait to implement many of them into my lesson plans this year."

B.M., Teacher, Brownsville Independent School District

"This was an eye-opener! I vow to work on changing myself. Thanks!"

J.C.M., Teacher, Northeast Independent School District

"This was a powerful message...You provide wonderful insight, personal testament, and solid illustrations...."

J.R., Principal, Uvalde Independent School District

"This has been the most effective training I have ever attended."

J.Z., Specials Teacher, Victoria Independent School District

"I wish all our in-services were as helpful as this material has been. Not only will this help at school, but in all areas of my life. Thanks again."

M.R., Teacher, Alice Independent School District

"This was awesome! It was scary how much of this information is EXACTLY what this school needs. I hope to see/ hear much more, and I hope everyone's ears were open!"

E. C. , Teacher, Coldspring-Oakhurst Consolidated Independent School District

"I've been teaching for twenty-six years, and this was probably the best and most useful workshop I've been to... your presentation was the most 'teacher friendly' I've heard. Please continue your work. EDUCATION NEEDS YOU."

B.W., Master Teacher, Dallas Independent School District

The Power of a Teacher

Adam L. Saenz

The Power of a Teacher

Published by:
Intermedia Publishing, Inc.
P.O. Box 2825
Peoria, Arizona 85380
www.intermediapub.com

ISBN 978-1-937654-60-3

Although the contents of my story are based on actual facts, names have been changed and events compressed.

For every teacher who wants to make a difference

(especially Mrs. JoeElla Exley, Mrs. Polly McRoberts, and Mrs. Sharon Brewer Stahli— three teachers who did just that).

Acknowledgements

Thank you, Texas Elementary Principal and Supervisor Association for the invitation to partner with you in service to our state's educators. It is because of you that Lou has found a voice; it is because of you that his voice has begun to be heard. Dr. Trae Kendrick and Mrs. Kirsten Hund, thank you for the honest feedback and encouragement along the way. Your input has been invaluable.

Dennis Welch, thank you for coming along-side early on and encouraging me to tell Lou's story.

I am indebted to the review crew: real, live teachers who took time they probably did not have to review and respond with keen insight to early versions of the manuscript. The end result is better because of your insight. Nick Reeves, Johanna Ortiz, Kara Socol, Sam Sáenz, Otha Graham, Aaron Hogan, Bridget Cooper, Stephanie Garner, Edith Schneider, Alice Bost, Susan Evans, Jeff Post, Kathryn Hardy, and Blake Reeves. Thanks also to Tina Sabuko, Doug Baker, and Maria Benavidez for sharing about the power teachers have had in your lives.

Thank you to my colleagues in clinical practice: James Deegear, Ph.D., Erin Sandoval, Ph.D., Becki Haynes, Ph.D., Nancy Price, L.P.C., and Lanice Chappell, L.P.C. Thanks also to my Texas A&M undergraduate interns, Kristen Diou and Katie Martin. Thank you, Karen Garcia and Karen Watt for being the outstanding office managers that you are. Outside my practice, I am also indebted to DeWayne Taylor, Ph.D. and Mary Barringer, Ph.D. for their roles in shaping my professional development.

Thad Norvell, thank you for your editorial contribution. You understand and convey meaning through writing like no one I know. I cherish your friendship, and I'm glad we office together.

Thank you, Joey McGee. Who knew a brown kid from the *barrio Mexicano* could share so much in common with a black kid from the 9th ward? Love you, bro. Live to cool.

Thank you, Community Church of Bryan/College Station, particularly the the Stolz, King, and Norvell families. Thank you for loving the Sáenz family so well.

Alisa, thank you for your questions. Mya, thank you for your courage. Isaiah, thank you for your self-discipline. Andrew, thank you for your creativity. My hope is that each of you approaches your education with the same posture you approach your life: remember that intelligence usually is a liability to the individual who is not teachable.

Kim, thank you for Alisa, Mya, Isaiah, and Andrew. In your heart, you have embraced both Adam and Lou. You are the Father's *agape* revealed to me.

Table of Contents

CHAPTER 1

A Case Study: The Sixth Grader in Handcuffs

Let's start here: select the student on your campus you would vote "Most Likely to End Up the Sixth-grader Handcuffed in the Back Seat of a Police Car for Possession of Marijuana and Arson." Depending on where you teach, there might be several potential candidates—all strongly qualified—competing for your selection right about now. It is not a lovely thought, I know, but bear with me. We're going somewhere with this. Have you selected the student? Don't read on until you have. Now hold that thought while I give a little context.

Where It All Began

In 2008, the Texas Elementary Principals and Supervisors Association (TEPSA) asked me to present in the Distinguished Lecture Series at their summer conference. The idea was for me to address behavior management—always an in-demand training topic for educators—in the context of this new educational dynamic we were all learning about called Response to Intervention (RtI). My session was titled, simply enough, *What You Need to Know About RtI and Behavior Management.* I concluded the session with a very brief case study: What would it look like to actually *implement* a behavioral intervention using an RtI framework with a sixth grader in trouble with the law for possession of marijuana and arson? As I read through the feedback forms after the workshop, I was surprised that the brief case study—only a very small part of my presentation—was

what seemed to have impacted the participants the most. My
decision to include the case study had been, frankly, almost an
afterthought.

TEPSA then brought me back for their summer conference
in 2009, and I led a workshop on behavior management entitled
I've Tried Everything and Nothing Has Worked... Now What?
This time, though, based on the feedback I had received from
my lecture the summer before, I placed much more emphasis on
the case study. I took time to flesh out details, and I gave the kid
a name: Lou.

How does a sixth-grader end up in handcuffs, anyway?
What were his parents doing or not doing at home?
What were his teachers doing or not doing at school?
At what point was a psychological evaluation
warranted?
Once the school did intervene, how would you even
begin to think about measuring progress in a case like
this?

Again, the feedback was quite encouraging, reinforcing the
idea that something about this particular case study resonated
with hope for teachers. I had no idea then, but that case study—
the sixth-grader in handcuffs—would be the start of *The Power
of a Teacher*.

The Challenge of Teaching

Now, back to your selection for Most Likely. Even though
I've never met this kid, let's see how closely I can describe your
Most Likely based on data alone. Demographically this sixth
grader is likely to be an African American or Hispanic male
from a lower-income single parent home whose family life is
characterized by varying degrees of chaos, interaction with the
legal system and, perhaps, Child Protective Services.

Psychologically, he is sorely lacking in self-control and
respect for boundaries, having learned to use physical and verbal

aggression and intimidation to get what he wants and avoid what he doesn't— "a chronically-engaged coercive response set" is how we might refer to it in psychobabble.

Interested in modifying his behavior? Great. Take your pick— reward system or punishment, carrot or stick. Either approach will be increasingly less effective in shaping his behavior because he is, with each passing semester, growing more able to detach himself from what he truly wants and from what he truly fears. Imposed consequences—favorable or unfavorable— become irrelevant.

Academically, he is functioning below grade level. He probably has been referred to the district's special education for a psychological evaluation. Once he starts receiving special education services, even with that help, he actually becomes less likely to close the academic gap between himself and his general education classmates, less likely than his general education classmates to eventually graduate, and more likely to be placed in an alternative school for students with conduct problems and/ or to be arrested.

Relationally he is impacting you physically, and I don't just mean the obvious hitting or kicking. When you see Most Likely, your heart rate elevates, your palms sweat, your breathing becomes shallow and accelerated, and the muscles in the back of your neck tense. In essence, your body has been conditioned to engage in fight-or-flight mode in response to his presence. And when you call Most Likely's guardian in a desperate attempt to collaborate in the problem-solving process, if the current phone number is still a working number, it doesn't matter anyway because the guardian has long-since memorized every number associated with any phone in the district and won't answer. If you're lucky, you'll get the opportunity to leave a voicemail that you know will never be returned.

Okay, so how close was I? I'd bet my Michael Jordan rookie card against a five dollar bill that on the days when you want to quit teaching, on the days when you're wondering whether this whole thing is really worth it, Most Likely has something to do with it.

Of course, it's not just Most Likely. Even when he has good days, your responsibilities as a teacher leave you with the myriad of other life-sucking demands that make you question your sanity for signing a contract to teach yet another year: lesson plans, staff meetings (with colleagues you wish weren't your colleagues), parent meetings (with parents who are eager to tell you why you're at fault), mediocre pay, little power in most decision-making processes, long days and nights. The list could go on.

It is precisely in the context of that stress that I want you to take time not just to read, but to absorb this book. The dilemma you face is that your vocation—your calling—as a teacher places you between competing realities: on the one hand, you have the power to truly impact and change students' lives, and on the other hand, those life-changing transactions occur in a broader professional context that has the potential to absolutely wear you down.

I believe this book offers a solution to that dilemma.

The Sixth-Grader in Handcuffs Revealed

Remember the case study I shared at TEPSA? The sixth grader in handcuffs who inspired us to consider your Most Likely? That sixth-grader was not a case study of a kid I saw for therapy. He was not a student I was called to evaluate in a school setting. He was not just a kid I knew growing up.

That sixth-grader was me: Adam Louis Sáenz. Or, in those days, Lou. Let me tell you my story and why it matters to you as a teacher.

My family lived in a working-class neighborhood on the southeast side of Houston near Hobby airport. My dad worked days at a gas station a few blocks from our house, and he worked nights loading freight onto eighteen-wheelers. My mom worked as a bank teller. It was by no means a life of luxury, but my parents managed to pay bills, keep food on the table, and take the family on the occasional day trip to Galveston. Life was pretty simple for my older brother, older sister, and me: go to school, come home and do homework, then play outside until the streetlights came on. Happy is the child whose parents provide, protect, and direct. I was a happy child.

I knew I would love school long before I was old enough to attend. I overheard my brother and sister tell my mom seemingly endless stories about school: what they learned or what they did at recess or a joke their teacher told. The night before my first day of kindergarten, I was so excited I couldn't sleep.

Kindergarten did not disappoint. My teacher was Mrs. Tholan. She was wise, kind, noble, firm, and angelic

My classmates and I were asking two questions about this new experience of being in a classroom and having a teacher. The first question was: *Does my teacher care about me?* The second question was: *Can I make my own rules?* Mrs. Tholan made it absolutely clear from day one that the answers to those questions were "yes" and "no," respectively.

Gary Welter cried every morning for the first three weeks of school—I'm talking bawled-his-eyes-out-and-snot-running-out-his-nose cried. It was like every day of school was the first day of school all over again for him. By the end of the second week, I was ready for him to get over it already (and so was most of the class—I knew this because I took it upon myself to ask them). Every day, though, Mrs. Tholan would patiently wait with him at the door, smile, give him a hug, and say, "We are your friends, Gary. We are so happy you are here today."

Yep. She cares.

Even though in my heart I knew Mrs. Tholan didn't have a class favorite, I was secretly jealous of Monica Severs, who seemed limitless in her capacity to impress Mrs. Tholan. If Monica wasn't writing the alphabet with penmanship the rest of us could only dream of, she was out at recess sharing cupcakes that she had cooked in her Easy-Bake oven. One day Monica was discovered to have "borrowed" Mrs. Tholan's markers, which Mrs. Tholan had repeatedly instructed us were off limits for students. When Mrs. Tholan confronted Monica, Monica claimed that the custodian must have put the markers in her desk. One thing Monica was *not* good at was lying. Mrs. Tholan gave her a single look, and Monica crumbled. We though Mrs. Tholan would let Monica slide, though, since Monica always seemed to be earning bonus points; surely she had enough credit to get by on this one. Mrs. Tholan would have no part of that. Rules were rules. She immediately summoned Monica to her desk and issued the consequence: Monica would have no morning or lunch recess. Monica was devastated. I don't remember her ever "borrowing" markers again.

Nope. I can't make my own rules.

Mrs. Tholan's consistency left no doubt in our hearts and no mystery in our minds about the nature of our relationship with her.

During the first week of school, Mrs. Tholan let each student borrow a book from her personal library, and I picked *Curious George Flies a Kite*. I was fascinated by the cover image: a monkey holding a huge yellow and white striped kite, which looked to me like a good story waiting to happen. Several times over the course of the next few weeks, Mrs. Tholan would ask me how the book was coming, and would I share with enthusiasm about the crazy things George would do—how he was constantly getting into trouble, and how no matter what George did, the man with the yellow hat was always kind to him.

At the end of the first six weeks, Mrs. Tholan stood before the class and announced that the class was to have a special treat. For the morning reading time, instead of Mrs. Tholan reading from our daily reader, Lou was going to read *Curious George Flies a Kite*. I was thrilled. It was a command performance, if

I do say so myself, and I nailed it, cover to cover. I felt capable and confident.

I sat next to Mrs. Tholan at lunch later that day. As we settled into our sandwiches, she looked at me and smiled: "Thank you for your contribution in class today, Lou. It was very special." Her words were life to me. I was convinced the world could not possibly be more right than it was at that moment. I *knew* I would love school.

I smiled back at Mrs. Tholan. "Thanks," I said. "You're a great teacher."

Early in the summer after first grade, I came home from the little league park and saw a moving truck parked in my driveway. Life as I knew it was about to change forever.

My parents were having marital problems, I would later discover, so they decided to move back to their hometown in the Rio Grande Valley, hoping that the proximity to their families would provide them enough support to endure. It didn't.

I came home from school one day early in third grade, and my dad was gone. The story I got from my mother was that my dad had moved back to Houston to find a job, and once he found one, he was going to come back and get us. I was relieved, honestly. I still hadn't adjusted to our new town, and I missed my friends in Houston. Days, weeks, then months passed. Finally, I think my mother grew tired of my asking her every day if she had heard from dad, and she told me the truth: he wasn't coming back to get us—he was just gone.

Before my dad left, my mom had been actively involved in our lives—continually asking questions about our school, our friends, our interests—the kinds of things moms seem to intuitively ask and do. When we had problems, we knew we could turn to her for help with anything from a tough homework problem to a skinned knee. After my dad left, though, my mother became preoccupied with trying to feed and clothe three children on a bank teller's salary as she also tried to deal with her own issues in the wake of losing her marriage. She disengaged from my life, no longer willing or able to keep up with my siblings and me. It felt like a double-whammy: my dad left, and then my mom, though still physically present, also was gone.

The realization devastated me. I developed what would become my main coping strategy for many years to follow: I did what was modeled for me, and I disengaged from everyone, including myself. Disengaging was a gradual process of learning to care less, hope less, believe less, and want less from life. By the end of fifth grade, I ended up gravitating toward older kids in the neighborhood who introduced me to drugs; living that close to the border, any drug was both readily available and very affordable. If disengaging was my new coping mechanism, drugs were my new escape.

As the summer before sixth grade came to a conclusion, serendipity paid me a visit. When my mother bought my school supplies, by accident she bought for me what was on my sister's list. Among the "accidental" purchases were three spiral notebooks. Though I didn't need them for school, I didn't tell her that and secretly kept them anyway. If my mom knew they weren't required for school, I felt sure she would return them for a refund. I knew every penny counted in our home, but I loved drawing and decided to squirrel them away for that purpose. Then something odd happened. One day, instead of drawing in them, I started writing in them. At first, I wrote poems and short stories, but eventually I began to write about my life. I found in those blank pages my only truly safe place to be honest—to be me. I had nowhere else to express the sense of loneliness and betrayal I felt, nowhere else to express the anger towards my parents. My anger turned into rage, and sadness turned into depression.

By the time sixth grade started, I didn't care who cared about me, and at school, I was asking only one of the two questions I asked Mrs. Tholan: *Can I make my own rules?* I had learned that disengaging was a two-edged sword. The cost of relational isolation was that I no longer was able to receive love or nurturing when it may have been offered. The benefit, though, was that

I was protected from experiencing emotional pain, or at least much more in control of the process. The isolation also offered me autonomy—breaking rules was so much easier when I wasn't worried about how my defiance affected my relationships with my teachers or my mother.

Mr. Smith was known among students as sort of an old-school, hard-nosed, in-your-face type, and he was keen on making sure I knew I could not make my own rules. After first period on the first day of sixth grade, Mr. Smith found me in the hallway and introduced himself.

"Lou, I've heard about you," he said to me sternly, leaning over, his nose into my face. "I know you vandalize property. I know you set fires. I know you use drugs. I know you've given your teachers a run for their money. I want you to know one thing from the start—it is my goal this year to get you in line, and I will not put up with any of your crap. Period. In fact, if you so much as even look at me wrong or speak a word of Spanish in my classroom, you, me, and this big brown paddle of mine will head down to the principal's office, and I *will* break you down. Do you understand me?"

I knew in an instant what this was about, and I responded accordingly: "*Sí entiendo, pendejo.*" (For my non-Spanish-speaking friends, "Yes, I understand, you !#$%*.") It was a short honeymoon.

It seemed my entire educational experience soon boiled down to me either walking to or from the principal's office. Profanity. Fights. Disrespect. Dress code violations. A few days' suspension. Then, then the cycle would start all over again. My teachers and I had developed behavioral expectations of each other, and most days, it felt like we were all operating on autopilot.

And so it went, day after day, week after week, month after month. Some days, Mr. Smith would win. Some days, I would win. By the Christmas holiday, though, both Mr. Smith and I were ready for a break from each other. Unfortunately, things weren't going too well at home, either—the usual conflicts and stressors, only with greater intensity. My time off campus was unstructured and unpredictable, and I became even more depressed, gaining momentum in a particularly unhealthy direction.

My new year started in January with the after-school detention I was scheduled to serve for my most recent pre-holiday infraction. I had arranged to meet with some older friends after detention to get high in a small, abandoned A-frame house near the edge of town. We just called it "the party house." To our surprise, the police arrived. When they heard our mad scramble inside, they drew weapons and surrounded us. My friend who was carrying most of the drugs fled on foot, but two other friends and I were cornered and handcuffed. It all happened so quickly; it felt surreal, like a dream. My head was spinning.

I still remember the pain of the handcuffs digging into my wrists as the officer loaded us into the back seat of the cruiser. I tried to stand with my feet on the floorboard and my shoulders on the top of the seat to keep the handcuffs from cutting into the top of my hands. Both my friends slumped forward in the back seat, hiding their faces as the officer took the long route to the station, through downtown, because he "wanted to take a joy-ride." At the juvenile detention facility, my older friends represented the possibility of access to the proverbial bigger fish for the police. As the youngest of the group, I was released, under certain parameters, to the custody of my mother.

Incidents like that can be a wake-up call. Rather than serving as a turning point, though, that event merely became a highlight of my ongoing decline. Things only got worse as the semester progressed, both for me individually and for my crowd. Two of my friends arranged to make a drug buy with the intent to rob the dealer. Unbeknownst to my friends, the "dealer" was an undercover officer, and they were caught in a sting. When my friends drew their guns for the robbery, they were both shot and killed.

At that time, there was little formal gang activity where I lived, but we all traveled in a few different packs and tried to stay loyal to each other. My friends' deaths shook up everyone. Accusations flew and tensions were high. A leader in the group I ran with did something (to this day, I don't know what) to offend one of our rival groups, and the retaliation was swift. I was the target of their revenge, and in retrospect, I assume it was because I was the youngest. Seven young men came to my house where two of my group and I were hanging out. They overpowered us, and they held me back as they tore the place apart. Worse by far, they forced me to watch as they sexually assaulted a girl I knew well. Whatever fragment was left of my ability to trust and my ability to be emotionally vulnerable was destroyed that day.

The next day, I hid the cuts and bruises, hid the pain, and none of us—including the victim of the sexual assault—ever told a soul. In retrospect, I'm baffled by the fact that I was back at school that next morning. It had been the same scenario the day after my friends died in the drug deal—we were back in school the next day, and no one spoke a word of it. There were no counselors to hold grief groups, nothing. What I experienced off campus in no way *excused* my behavior on campus, but it certainly did *explain* much of it. To be very clear, I absolutely believe my inappropriate behavior needed consequences. As I look back, though, I wonder if my teachers would have understood and approached me differently if they had some clue about what my life was like off campus.

Even in my journals, there are very few allusions to the events of those months. I think they were simply too painful and confusing to acknowledge or explore writing. What is clear now, though, is that the trauma of those months re-shaped the core of my identity. All the evidence in my life pointed me to the single, undeniable conclusion that I was inadequate. I was an inadequate son. I was an inadequate student. I was an inadequate friend. I had long since forgotten the capable and confident Lou that sat in Mrs. Tholan's kindergarten class, and I was firmly entrenched in my new identity: a drug-using, depressed vandal from a single parent home.

By that point, my mother knew things didn't look good for me. Desperate to salvage my remaining childhood years, she found a way out for me. A family friend—he and his wife were teachers—heard of my difficulties and offered to take me in. Although Child Protective services was not involved with our family, my mother signed a permanent transfer of guardianship, and within a matter of days, I was living with a new family, several hundred miles away from all I had come to know.

———————

The change was dramatic. In my new home I was loved well. I didn't have to worry about food, clothes, or my personal safety. I didn't want anyone at this new school to know about my past. I was very careful not to talk about it and simply do my best to blend in—not an easy road for a Hispanic with my background suddenly in school with predominantly upper-middle class white students. The subject didn't come up often, but when my friends asked about why I wasn't living with my parents, I gave vague responses. Everyone extended grace by not prying.

Through junior high and high school, I stayed out of trouble and was socially engaged. I even made decent grades. I wasn't using drugs, and I managed to spend most of my time with peers who cared about school. In reality, though, I simply shifted from being the Lou who was outwardly defiant to the Lou who was outwardly compliant, but inwardly desperate. The waves of depression continued. An entry from my journal:

October 27, 1982…

"I don't understand it. There's just this darkness all around. I can't get past it. I never know when it's going to show up, and when it comes, it stays for days."

I dreaded high school graduation. The family I was living with had been very good to me, but when I turned eighteen and graduated, I knew I would be on my own. I had a sneaking suspicion that the demons from my past—which really had only teased me throughout high school—were patiently waiting to do real damage once I was living independently.

Just as I feared, after I graduated and moved out on my own, the bottom fell out. I had struggled with depression for many years, but now I also was beginning to experience symptoms of anxiety—sleep difficulties, racing thoughts, and heart palpitations. Once again, I turned to street drugs to self-medicate. I had no real sense of the future; I simply hoped to make it through each day.

I was sleeping on the living room floor of a co-worker's apartment, and everything I owned fit in the bottom half of his hallway closet. My journals were my most valued possession. One evening, after a particularly dark day, I found myself alone in the apartment reading through these records of my life. As I opened one of the journals, two pieces of paper fell out—letters written to me by two of my high school English teachers just before graduation. These are excerpts from each letter:

> "You are extremely talented and intelligent, but most importantly, you have a good heart... I know you will use your talents to help your fellow man, and that is the most satisfying life that a person can have." -Jo Ella Exley

> "Don't quit writing (especially in your journal). Someday it may be the basis for your book... you have insight, sensitivity, intelligence, and maturity beyond your tender years... keep on analyzing and thinking— you are so adept at it. Most of all, keep on being you. You are a special person." -Polly McRoberts

Until that night, I had completely forgotten about these letters. Yet, as I sat there reading and rereading them, lonely, anxious, and mired in depression, something clicked. I thought back to my experiences in Mrs. Exley's and Mrs. McRoberts's classes: I knew they cared, and I knew I couldn't make my own rules. I also knew they were honest. They would not write anything to me that they didn't truly believe, and I knew I could trust them. In that moment, somehow, I simply chose to take them at their word, and I accepted their assessment of me. For the first time in a very long time— maybe ever—I believed that their words about me might be true. I was done being Lou. Just for emphasis—if only for myself—I decided I would start going by my first name: Adam. It was time.

I enrolled in one college course: Introduction to English at the University of Texas at San Antonio. Immediately, though, I was overwhelmed with fear: How would I pay for tuition or books? How would I get to class? Even after discovering financial aid, I was attacked by fear again when I actually stepped on campus. I felt like an obvious imposter. What business did I have on a college campus? What did I possibly have in common with these other students, all of whom seemed so much younger than me and whom must have come from healthy, well-adjusted families? I overheard animated conversations about vacation plans for spring break (I would be working double shifts at the restaurant to pay for tuition—very uncool. *I'm out*). I overheard conversations about pledging fraternities (Word was that you had to pay to get into one, and most fraternity guys I saw didn't dress like they shopped at thrift stores—at least not the one I did. *I'm out*). I kept to myself that first semester and focused on work and Introduction to English.

At the end of that first semester, I received a letter from the university: I passed Introduction to English! I could not believe it. I decided to take a second class just to rule out the possibility that my passing Introduction to English was a clerical error. At the end of that second semester, I received another letter from the university. I passed again! My second college class, done! After years of working full-time and taking a few classes each semester, I received yet another letter, this one from the Registrar's Office: I actually would graduate with a Bachelor of Arts in English. I was almost twenty-seven years old.

The following years were filled with more school—a master's degree in counseling, a Ph.D. in school psychology from Texas

A&M, clinical training Harvard Medical School, and a post doctorate from the Alpert Medical School at Brown University.

There's an inside joke in my profession that the real reason we entered the field was to work on our own issues. That was certainly the case for me. As I started coursework for my masters program, I was hoping to try to make some sense of my life up to that point, and I realized I needed individual counseling. The effects of trauma don't just go away, and I knew that certain memories still held a grip on my mind and my heart.

I felt psychologically raw for weeks after each session. There were days I wondered whether I was actually getting worse than better—days I didn't want to go to work, days I didn't want to go to class, days I didn't want to be around another human being, and days I felt absolutely miserable regardless of whether I took my medication. Being honest with myself and talking about my thoughts and feelings—session after painful session—was like a series of broken bones finally being reset. The process was not at all pleasant, but it was essential for my proper healing and growth.

In the end, I found truth, and it set me free: My parents' divorce? Not my fault, not my responsibility. My friends' murder? Not my fault, not my responsibility. The sexual assault? Not my fault, not my responsibility. My future—the rest of my life and what happens to me? No one else's fault, wholly my responsibility. After all I had been through, the greatest challenge was still ahead: could I be vulnerable again? Could I trust that the healing power of love was worth the risk that accompanies vulnerability?

I could write about how teachers impact their students from a variety of perspectives: sociologically, behaviorally, pedagogically, culturally, and so on. I want to focus on the teacher's role in shaping a child's identity, which might be thought of as the culminating effect of each of those perspectives.

People in my field take entire graduate courses on personality and identity development, so for the sake of brevity, let me borrow some wisdom from PBS's *Antiques Roadshow*. The show's website describes it as "part adventure, part history lesson, and part treasure hunt." The premise is simple: take your item to the appraiser and let him tell you whether you have a valuable antique or junk. My favorite vignettes are ones in which the owner thinks she has an item that is junk that, upon appraisal, is found to be of great value: "My husband uses this lamp in the basement for his workshop, but I've always wondered where it came from. We bought it at a garage sale in 1982 for five bucks." Then, the appraiser will discuss the item's distinguishing qualities and conclude with something like, "This is an excellent example of this series. If it were to come up at auction, I would estimate its value at $60,000. You should probably get it insured for that amount, and by all means, get it out of your husband's workshop."

I love those moments because they remind me of a very simple, but fundamental human truth—one that is crucial for teachers to know and remember. In a nutshell, that truth is this: identity and perceived value impact function and behavior. If I believe my lamp is worth five bucks, I will treat it like a five-dollar lamp. If I believe it is worth $60,000, I will insure it, protect it, and invest myself in its preservation. The same is true for people. If I believe myself to be of little value, I behave accordingly. If, however, I believe myself to be valuable—to have the ability to matter to the world around me—I live as though my choices matter. The corollary is true as well.

The feedback loop, then, is that how I perceive and understand myself play a critical role in the choices I make about my behavior. How I behave, in turn, impacts how others respond to me. How others respond to me, then, impacts how I perceive and understand myself. Over time, we tend to commit to an identity. We prefer and default to the behavioral feedback loop that offers the least cognitive dissonance—the one that aligns with and reinforces the identity with which we are most comfortable and believe to be true, regardless of how inaccurate we may be in our self-assessment.

Until I truly absorbed what Mrs. Exley and Mrs. McRoberts were communicating to me in those letters, my feedback loop reinforced my sense that I lacked value, thereby undermining my sense of purpose. I desperately needed something (or someone) to step into my chaos and clarify my value. I have no idea what Mrs. Exley or Mrs. McRoberts were doing that night as I sat in a quiet apartment, but months after their active investment in me, their words convinced me of my value. They gave me the courage to step out of years of a deeply rooted fear that I would forever be Lou, the kid who gets high and gets handcuffed, and step into who I might become if they were right about me. I needed their encouragement to hope that a different life was possible. I needed their encouragement to take the first of what became the many steps out of a false identity and into whom I have now become.

I'll finish my mini-autobiography with one final story.

Several years into my private practice, I wanted to develop a model to treat anxiety disorders that incorporates both psychological and spiritual aspects of the patient's being. I enrolled in a Doctorate of Ministry program at Graduate Theological Foundation, and for my thesis, I completed a short-term residency at the Christ Church College of Oxford University.

A highlight of my time at Oxford was the high table dinner in The Great Hall (Harry Potter fans, think Hogwarts Dining Hall). The high table dinner is a long-standing tradition at Oxford in which faculty dine with their students at a table—raised on a platform—located at the end of the dining hall. I was assigned a seat next to my instructor, Canon Vincent Strudwick, who had recently been awarded the prestigious Lambeth Degree by the Archbishop of Canterbury. While it was clear after the first hour in Canon Strudwick's class that he was fantastically brilliant, what I appreciated most about him was his meek and gentle spirit; it would be hard to be in his class and not feel loved. Still, I felt somewhat out-of-place as a psychologist in a classroom filled with seasoned clergy from around the world.

As we settled into the entrée of our four-course meal, Canon Strudwick looked at me and smiled.

"Thank you for your contribution to the class discussion, Dr. Sáenz," he encouraged me in his high British accent. "As a psychologist, you bring us a unique perspective. It's refreshing for us theologians, and I believe it makes our shared experience in the classroom all the richer."

In an instant, I flashed back to the meal I had shared with Mrs. Tholan thirty-five years before—a memory I had long since forgotten. I was immediately overwhelmed by a flood of emotion, and I fought the lump in my throat. "Thank you for saying so, Canon Strudwick," I managed to respond. Then I smiled and added, "You're a great teacher."

Why I Wrote *The Power of a Teacher*

Statistically speaking, I am an "outlier." Outliers are bits of data that don't end up on the data grid where we think they ought to, based on how the variables we're observing have interacted in past cases. Outliers can be something of a flashing dashboard light that prompt us to wonder what happened, specifically, to make this one piece of data end up way over here, alone, when the rest of the data set is huddled way over there, nicely and predictably, where we expected it to huddle. When we pay attention to outliers, we stand to learn more about the cause-and-effect relationships among the variables we are observing.

I didn't realize it at the time, but when I shifted in that TEPSA workshop from presenting research to simply sharing my story, the session became less about the knowledge and information I could offer educators as Dr. Sáenz and more about the encouragement I could offer educators as Lou, a kid whose life was deeply impacted and whose direction was profoundly changed by teachers.

The take-away lesson for me as a psychologist and trainer was clear: while teachers may need additional knowledge and information to be effective (RtI today, who-knows-what next year), most of all teachers need hope. They need a reason to believe, or maybe they just need a reminder, that it really *is* worth their while to invest their resources—their time, their money, their energy, their relationships, their lives—not just in teaching, but in teaching well. In 2010, the global financial institution ING conducted a survey in conjunction with the National Teacher of the Year Award. They found that eighty-eight percent the 1,000 Americans age eighteen and older who were surveyed identified at least one teacher who had a significant, positive impact on their life. Ninety-eight percent believed that a good teacher can change the course of a student's life. In fact, teachers were second only to immediate family as the group having the greatest, positive impact on the lives of those surveyed as they grew up—even ahead of close friends.

So, what began as a case study at a workshop evolved into the book you are now holding in your hands. As an outlier whose life trajectory was forever changed by teachers who cared, I wanted to write a book to encourage educators, to remind them of their power (both in the lives of the students they teach and in their own lives), and to equip them to maintain the wellness and balance in their lives that will empower them to live into the greatest potential of their calling.

What to Expect

I want you to teach from a place of wellbeing. What I've realized working with clients in both private practice and school settings is that when we don't maintain wellbeing in critical areas of our lives, we—to again put it in psychobabble— "decompensate," which refers to a breakdown in the coping systems we keep in place to make our lives function. At the point of decompensation, information and knowledge about what we should be doing to live effectively become increasingly useless; the further we slide into a state of decompensation, the more we lack the capacity to actually do what we know we should do. The vicious cycle: As we decompensate, we become less effective. As we become less effective, we become more anxious. As we become more anxious, we decompensate even further. On and on the cycle continues. The teacher caught in this cycle is at-risk for losing touch with the profound vocational calling to impact students' lives, tragically trading it for not much more than a willingness to tolerate the job because it provides a paycheck and benefits with summers off.

How do we break the decompensation cycle? We return to— or find for the first time—a place of personal wellness.

The Power of a Teacher is a wellness guide designed to help you find balance and peak experience in your role as a teacher. After you read about the five core areas of wellbeing, you'll take The Teacher Wellness Inventory, a fifty-item assessment designed specifically for teachers that measures wellbeing in the occupational, emotional, financial, spiritual, and physical areas of your life. The assessment reveals to what degree you are living a balanced life and identifies areas of weakness to target for growth.

Change—even change for the better—can be overwhelming. Not to worry. You'll read about the psychological dynamics that maximize your ability to make the changes you need. The Change Organizer will guide you through a step-by-step process of prioritizing goal-setting and establishing support and accountability in the areas of your life that need attention.

In addition to the Teacher Wellness Inventory and the Change Organizer, discussion questions are included at the end of each chapter with the hope of creating dialogue and building professional community among you and your colleagues— maybe an exercise for you and your co-teacher, maybe for the teachers at your grade level, maybe for your entire campus. A quick note about the discussion questions: my experience leading group discussions tells me that most people don't like going first when answering question like these, so I decided I would go first. After each question, I have written my responses, being as vulnerable and brutally honest as I know how to be. You get to go second, and I hope you will find the courage to be honest with yourself and your colleagues.

Finally, at the end of each of the five chapters about specific areas of wellbeing, you will read a brief story about someone whose life was changed by a teacher. These are the encouraging stories I worry teachers don't hear enough of—stories that real lives are changed by real teachers who understand and live out their calling.

In my years of working in school systems, I have observed that when a teacher is well—not just free of obvious symptoms, but truly functioning at optimum capacity—variables like student behavior, parental involvement, teaching strategies, and test scores, while certainly relevant, will not ultimately control the quality or effectiveness of the professional experience. Those realities won't disappear, of course, but a healthy teacher can navigate them, confident that the goal of his or her vocation—impacting students—still is well within reach.

We who have been impacted by the power of a teacher know the crucial role educators play in shaping the future. To all teachers who read this book: Be encouraged. Be enlightened. Be well.

JoElla Exley Elementary, Katy Independent School District

Polly McRoberts Elementary, Katy Independent School District

"Life is not merely to be alive, but to be well."

~Marcus Valerius Martial

CHAPTER 2

The Case for Wellness

unbalancedteacher.blogspot.com
November 11, 2011
10:49 p.m.

I need to vent.

I'm glad all you know about me is that I'm a teacher, and I'm going to hide in the anonymity of this blog and be brutally (offensively?) honest. I realize that exactly half of you who subscribe to this blog, once offended, could find me easily if you wanted—you know my name, my address, and my cell number— but that half of you is my mom, and she only checks her e-mail about twice during any given presidential term.

Okay, here it goes…

I couldn't sleep last night. I hate to admit it, but I'm worried sick about how my fifth-grade class is going to do on the math portion of the standardized test this coming April. And it's only November :(

Since I stayed up late last night, I slept late this morning, and by the time I managed to get the kids dressed and dropped off at school, I had just enough time to swing by Starbucks. I could tell that today was going to be an iced-peppermint-white-mocha-with-an-extra-shot-of-espresso kind of day. Whole milk and whipped cream. Venti. I know, I know—not exactly health food, but I'm finally willing to admit I've lost the battle with my weight. I'm tired of the diet roller coaster routine and the reality that my "after" pictures always end up looking worse than my "before" pictures (like I really have time to work out, anyway). Fortunately, by the time I made it to campus, the caffeine was starting to kick in, so I was able to get some juices flowing.

Earlier this week we started a math unit on word problems, combining multiple skills in the same problem. Based on what I saw in the kids' performance today, I'm pretty sure I'm not getting the concepts across. (Sample problem: There are 3 types of sundae toppings—chocolate chips, colored sprinkles, and smarties. How many different types of sundaes are possible with the three different toppings? You may have 1, 2 or 3 toppings; their answers: "9BR43" "i luv iscreme" "1, 2 or 3 toppings").

Part of the issue is that I have a handful of English language learners in my class this year, and I never even thought to go to any kind of workshop or professional development to prepare me how to teach them. They're all really sweet, and I feel so bad because I just don't quite know how to connect with them. Another part of the problem is that I have three kids whose sole mission in my class is to destroy education everywhere. Unlike the English language learners, these three kids are not exactly sweet. One of them has a moustache.

Every time I look at my lesson plans, I feel panic—my heart races and I can feel my body getting tense. When it's really bad, I get these headaches that last for two days.

I had my usual energy crash around 1:30 this afternoon. You know the feeling? Like when you get to the point where you're present physically, but you have absolutely no mental or emotional energy to give. I call it "zombie mode."

And, of course, zombie-mode was exactly when Donna decided to stick her head into my classroom. I just don't get her. She's been teaching for over fifteen years. Has the thought ever occurred to her that I might need some help or some guidance or something? Then again, even if she offered, I'm not sure I'd accept it from her. I've overheard her in the workroom talking about how she "can't believe what a zoo Miss Macy's class is," and how "Mrs. Spencer has been such a show-off since she won the lead teacher award last year." She's so catty, and what makes it even worse is that she has a way of gathering everyone on her side. So, when she popped her head into my classroom this afternoon, I didn't even want to deal with her. I can't even remember what she said, honestly. I just said, "Yeah, okay," and hoped that she and her bad hair-do would leave. Call me crazy, but sometimes I honestly don't know who I can trust and who I can't on this campus—maybe I've just been stabbed in the back one too many times.

Today is definitely one of those days I'm pretty sure I don't get paid enough to put up with this. Even if I didn't have to put up with this, I'm still pretty sure I don't get paid enough. My credit cards are all almost maxed out, and for the past three months I've only made the minimum payments. We've talked about taking a road trip back home for Christmas, but I don't see how we're going to be able to afford it. Sorry, Mom. (Wait, by the time Mom reads this, this Christmas will be two Christmases ago.) So, um, sorry that we didn't make it for Christmas 2011, Mom. I hope you like the gift card we e-mailed you (that you got when you checked your e-mail three months after Christmas) since we couldn't afford to be there in person.

Why can't my life just be like Kim's? Perfect husband? Check. Perfect kids? Check. Perfect figure? Check. Perfect clothes and makeup? Check. Perfect house? Check. Dream vacations? Check. Not a teacher? Check.

I'm honestly thinking about switching careers. I don't know, maybe banking or real estate. I'm even thinking about following through with the rescue of that Nigerian prince being held captive who has several millions in a bank account, half of which he will gladly share with me if I will just forward him the small fee for his escape. He e-mailed again yesterday.

Seriously, though. Why am I doing this?

Is this where the sidewalk ends? Where do I go from here?

Well, now it's 11:16 p.m. Looks like it's going to be another late night. Thanks for reading.

—*Jennifer*

Meet the Teacher

Which part of Jennifer's story strikes closest to home: too busy to prepare to fully engage students academically or behaviorally (let alone finding time to exercise and eat right)? Relationally-isolated at work and carrying emotional baggage that prevents you from really connecting? Barely able to get by financially? In the end, wondering why you ever decided to become a teacher or whether you want to continue in the profession?

You, my teacher friend, are one of 7.2 million teachers in public school classrooms across the United States (as of the 2010 U.S. Census). You and your 7,199,999 colleagues make up the country's largest professional workforce. The United States Bureau of Labor and Statistics lists your average salary in the low-fifties—about $100,000 less than your child's pediatrician and about $35,000 more than the dishwasher at your favorite restaurant. The projected salary growth for your field is about as fast as average, which is between seven and thirteen percent in the next ten years.

One other thing: half of you will be employed in another profession after five years.

Why?

Burnout's Dashboard Lights

Christina Maslach, a professor of psychology at the University of California Berkeley,

has spent the last thirty years studying occupational burnout, and she has identified three key "dashboard lights" that tell us when it's time to check under the hood of the vehicle we call our vocation: emotional exhaustion, depersonalization, and reduced personal accomplishment. For the teacher, these three dashboard lights show up as the internal voice saying, "I'm *always* tired, I don't want to deal with the bag of idiots that are my colleagues, and I'm not making a difference in kids' lives anyway."

When we get to this stage of burnout, our tendency is to look for relief in changing our external circumstances. If only we could find the right campus. If only we could find the right administration. If only we could find parents who are invested in their child's education.

If only.

If ever someone had a reason for flashing dashboard lights and if-onlys, it would be Mihaly Csikszentmihalyi (his last name is pronounced, *"Chick-sent-me-HIGH-ee")*. As a child, Csikszentmihalyi's life was forever disrupted by World War II when his Hungarian family was living in Italy during the war. Csikszentmihalyi was held in an Italian prison camp while many of his family and friends were killed in Budapest.

Eventually, he found himself turning to art and chess as an escape.

"I discovered chess was a miraculous way of entering into a different world where [the atrocities of war] didn't matter. For hours I'd just focus within a reality that had clear rules and goals. If you knew what to do, you could survive there." As a teenager, Csikszentmihalyi became fascinated with psychology: "I'd seen something drastically wrong with how adults—the grown-ups I trusted—organized their thinking. I was trying to find a better system to order my life."

He began to study the works of Austrian psychiatrist Sigmund Freud and Swiss psychiatrist Carl Jung, and at the age of twenty-two, moved to the United States to study psychology. He arrived to Chicago with $1.25 in his pocket and was accepted to study psychology at the University of Chicago (that is, to study psychology *in English*, which was his fourth language and in which he had limited fluency). Csikszentmihalyi spent his years at the University of Chicago (and subsequent career) studying happiness and creativity.

So, after profound personal loss and struggle, what was Csikszentmihalyi's take on happiness?

> "The foremost reason that happiness is so hard to achieve is that the universe was not designed with the comfort of human beings in mind... it seems that every time a pressing danger is avoided a new and more sophisticated threat appears on the horizon... whether we are happy depends on inner harmony, not on the

controls we are able to exert over the great forces of the universe."

That is powerful, but what does that have to do with your role as a teacher? Let's go back to the last line of that quotation. This time, though, let's substitute a few phrases and try this:

"Whether I am happy depends on my personal wellness, not on how underfunded my campus is, how clueless my principal is, how catty my coworkers are, or how disengaged my students seem."

Think about that for a moment. As a teacher, you can invest your energy to affect external change: legislative change, demographic change, administrative change, fill-in-the-blank change. To a certain degree, such an investment in external variables is both helpful and necessary. The challenge, though, is that if we focus too much of our energy and intention on variables over which we have little control, we soon begin to feel and believe that we are powerless. Feelings and beliefs of hopelessness soon follow.

While Jennifer and the frustrations she vents in her blog may come across more as a caricature or negative stereotype of a struggling teacher, each element of struggle is based on real issues I have encountered in my consultation with teachers. The point of the blog is not to frame the teacher's role or experience in a negative or defeatist tone, but to let you know that in the context of this book, it's okay to be honest with yourself about whatever struggles you may be experiencing as a teacher. As one administrator noted, the concerns addressed in Jennifer's blog are "the truths [teachers] rarely speak of for fear of judgment."

My goal is to give you a roadmap to walk in power. The power and influence that you wield in the lives of your students begins with the power and influence you wield over your own life. That process starts with honesty—*what's not working in my life as a teacher, and how do I change it?*

Wellness: The Burnout Antidote

Wellness—both the term itself and the idea the term represents—while common in eastern medicine, is a fairly new concept to us westerners. The concept of wellness centers on proactively nurturing wellbeing, versus reactively treating illness as symptoms arise. The idea is that if we spend a concentrated bit of our attention taking care of ourselves, the frequency, intensity, and duration of illness will decrease significantly; in terms of our psychological functioning, maintaining wellness is our first defense against stress and burnout.

Table 1 summarizes key differences between eastern and western approaches to medicine; in general, the eastern model emphasizes holistic prevention via natural sources, while the western model focuses on treating specific symptoms via medication or surgery. As the table illustrates, both medical models are valuable to our overall wellbeing.

	Eastern Model	Western Model
Focus	Holistic (macro). Views mind and body as connected and interactive	Atomistic (micro). Views mind and body as distinct treatment targets
Perspective	Views the being as a garden; physician as gardener seeking to cultivate life	Views the being as a machine; physician as mechanic seeking to fix/ replace broken parts
Goal	Maintain state of balance and wellbeing	Maintain the absence of symptoms
Strengths	Self-care; prevention; natural treatments with few side-effects	Handling trauma; life-threatening illnesses; diagnostic accuracy

Table 1: Eastern and Western Models of Medicine

The World Health Organization defines health as "a state of complete physical, occupational and social well-being, and not merely the absence of disease or infirmity." What I love about this definition is that it reminds us that the true litmus test of wellbeing is not the absence of identifiable stressors in any area of our life—occupational, emotional, financial, spiritual, or physical—but our ability to effectively cope with those stressors as they arise.

Think back to the analogy in Table 1: the eastern perspective of individuals as a garden. Let's expand the analogy and think of schools as gardens. In gardening, the way to make the widest variety of plants grow over time is not to feed the various plants, but to feed the soil. Our schools are faced with the challenge of academically and behaviorally growing children from a wide variety of ethnic, cultural, linguistic, cognitive, and socioeconomic backgrounds. Our staff is the soil into which these seeds are planted.

What is true in families is also true in schools: the first effective intervention for all children is an adult living a balanced, healthy life. Even the best academic and behavioral interventions, when implemented by staff on the verge of burnout, will have minimal positive effect.

Research Shows…

Sounds good in theory: healthy adults—by definition—live balanced lives, make good choices, and make good schools. But can we find any scientific evidence to support the idea that healthy individuals make healthy organizations?

Yes.

In 2008, the Center for Disease Control and Prevention conducted a study in conjunction with the Capital Metropolitan Transportation on Authority in Austin. Capital Metro faced two challenges. First, the company was swamped by the rising costs of health care; second, employee morale was in the tank. The company implemented a wellness program that included incentives for employees to access healthier food options, wellness workshops, dietary counseling, smoking cessation programs and a fitness center. Employees also were encouraged to create partnerships with their colleagues for accountability and support.

The result? Participants reported improvements in physical activity, healthy food consumption, weight loss, and blood pressure. Absenteeism decreased by 25 percent, a greater sense of community and morale was reported, and the company's overall health care costs were dramatically reduced.

"Ah, yes," you say. "But that's in Austin—the hipster Mecca of Texas. Could those results have been possible in my school, which is located squarely in The Land That Time Forgot ISD?"

"Absolutely," John Allegrante would answer. He and his colleagues in the Department of Health Education at the Teachers College of Columbia University studied the effects of a similar program implemented in ten inner-city schools. Their findings were similar to those of the CDC study in Austin. When staff invested the effort to pursue wellness, the net results included greater staff cohesion, a greater sense of shared mission, and more favorable relationships between the teachers and students.

The Five Areas of Wellbeing

Each of the next five chapters is written to give an overview of key issues regarding occupational, emotional, financial, spiritual, and physical wellbeing. Keep in mind that the five areas are interconnected, which means limitations in any given area will, in turn, negatively impact the other five areas. For example, if I experience stress due to my lack of financial wellbeing, I can be sure that the stress will bleed into my emotional wellbeing, which, in turn, has the potential to negatively impact my physical wellbeing.

Volumes already have been written on each area of wellbeing, and it is not the purpose of this book to serve as a comprehensive guide to occupational, emotional, financial, spiritual, or physical wellbeing. You're a teacher, and I understand the demands on your time. I've narrowed the focus to two or three keys: what you absolutely need to know in a nutshell. I arrived at these keys based on my research and experience in clinical practice. In essence, the keys are the nuggets that offer you the most bang-for-the-buck as you invest in your wellbeing.

As we explore each of the five areas, we will turn to Jennifer as an ongoing case study. We will review the results of her Teacher Wellness Inventory to see what is not working in her life, and we will review her Change Organizer to see what changes she is going to make to get herself to a point of teaching—and hopefully living—from her sweet spot. Jennifer's situation may seem both overwhelming and hopeless. When we feel overpowered by adversity and hardship, too often we fail to make any progress at all, realizing that no one solution can change everything. What we forget in those moments is that most large problems aren't solved by one solution, but by many small solutions over time. I created Jennifer (and her pile of problems) quite purposefully, wanting to illustrate that in the face of such dire circumstances, she—and ultimately you—can affect meaningful change one small step at a time.

My goal to help shift your understanding of the stressors you face as a teacher into a broader context—a context that is mindful of variables over which you do have control and variables which you do not. As a teacher, your profession is wrought with squeaky wheels—students, parents, curriculum, administration, federal guidelines, and on and on. The teacher intent on a lifetime journey on the road of education is wise to consistently invest meaningful quantities of the oil of his or her attention on the wheel that matters most: the wheel of personal wellbeing. You do have power to make lives better, including your own.

So yes, there is still bad news: you teach in a system over which you have very little absolute control. But fortunately, that is only the headline, and the full story is—or can be—much more encouraging than the headline we read every day.

Conclusion

What you already know has been proven with actual data. In 2007, a study conducted by The National Center for Educational Statistics cited a key variable in explaining teacher turnover: teachers felt burned out because so much was expected from them in a system in which they had so little control. A primary benefit of the self-reflection you will experience through the Teacher Wellness Inventory is that it will provide you a format to focus your attention and energy on the variables you *can* control: those key internal variables that truly drive your life experience.

In the end, we'll find that Saturday Night Live character Stewart Smalley was right: It's a lot easier to put on a pair of slippers than to carpet the whole world.

Summary

- There are three primary characteristics of burnout: 1) feeling chronically tired; 2) depersonalizing our coworkers (or students or parents); and 3) feeling that we're not making a difference.

- When we're at burnout, our tendency is to look to external and relatively uncontrollable variables (the campus, the students, the parents, the administration, etc.) to find relief.

- The treatment for burnout is to nurture wellness, which is the process of focusing on internal, controllable variables to create change. When we're experiencing a lack of wellness in one area of our life, that lack will negatively affect the other areas.

- Wellness is characterized not by the absence of stress (physical, emotional, occupational, spiritual, or financial), but by the ability to effectively cope with stress and thrive.

Questions for Discussion

1. When you need to vent, who's your best listener?

   First is my wife, Kim. Then, my friend Eric Kelley.

2. Would you rather have a free week off or a bonus of two weeks' salary? What would you do with your choice?

   I'd take the free week and work on my 1966 Ford F100. I'd probably install hydraulics and drop it two inches off the ground, add spinners, ground effects and a fifteen-inch subwoofer.

3. What's your worry dream?

   My worry dream is that I'm at the park with my wife and kids when I suddenly realize I have a final the next day, and I completely forgot I was even taking a class. Only in the past year am I beginning to remember, in my dream, that I already have a Ph.D., and it really doesn't matter if I fail another class.

4. What's the hardest part of your job?

   Dealing with managed care (A.K.A. insurance companies). Don't get me started.

5. Talk about a time you felt really alive.

   I think it's this very season of my life. Physically, I'm finally eating clean and exercising, not because I want to look good, but as an act of wise stewardship of my body. Before now, I had taken my body for granted for way too long. Emotionally, I'm learning to let others speak into my life in love, trusting that it's time to let go of the anger I've harbored about my past. I think letting go of the anger has made space in my heart for me to love my wife and four children more deeply and with greater sacrifice. Professionally, it's been a joy to write this book—something that's been on my heart to do for many years. I'm also realizing my limits as a therapist and trying to build my caseload accordingly. Spiritually, completing the coursework and thesis for my D.Min. has, as my tutor Canon Vincent Strudwick at Oxford University noted, "stretched me to the corner posts of my faith." Not necessarily a pleasant experience, but critical in my spiritual journey. Financially... hmm. Still growing here. It's not like the lights are going to get shut off this month, but I still worry about getting four kids through college, paying for two weddings, and all that other later-in-life stuff.

"There are countless studies on the negative spillover of job pressures on family life, but few on how job satisfaction enhances the quality of family life."

~Albert Bandura

CHAPTER 3

OCCUPATIONAL WELLBEING

"Part of the issue is that I have a handful of English language learners in my class this year, and I never even thought to go to any kind of workshop or professional development to prepare me how to teach them…[Donna] is a 'master teacher,' but has the thought ever occurred to her that I might need some help or some guidance or something? Then again, even if she offered, I'm not sure I'd accept it from her. I've overheard her in the workroom talking about how she 'can't believe what a zoo Miss Macy's class is,' and how 'Mrs. Spencer has been such a show-off since she won the lead teacher award last year.' She's so catty, and what makes it even worse is that she has a way of gathering everyone on her side."

The teacher who is not experiencing occupational wellbeing invests a substantial portion of each day's life energy—weekends included—into an endeavor that will offer in return theft of leisure time and relational isolation. If I am that teacher, it will only be a matter of time before I develop deep resentment for my job.

Are you that teacher? If so, your hope lies in the reality that you have power to create and maintain professional relationships with your colleagues that can be a rich emotional and intellectual resource to you, and vice-versa. Also, that hope is part of the larger reality that you really do have power to find fulfillment both on and off campus.

What is Occupational Wellbeing?

We are bombarded daily by magazine covers, commercials, and new books offering us the secret to personal happiness. Words like "wellness" can lose their meaning in a hurry, so I want to be careful to avoid vague ideas of happiness and keep us focused on a fairly specific target. Occupational wellness, according to wellness researcher David Anspaugh, is simply "the ability to achieve a balance between work and leisure time." Occupational wellness involves learning to deal with workplace stress, building stronger working relationships with your co-workers, exploring options to create a better work environment, and progressing toward your career goals.

Steve Dinham, researcher for the Australian Council for Educational research, surveyed teachers from Australia, New Zealand, and England and found that across all three countries, teachers noted the following common challenges: increased community criticism, lower teacher status, and lack of control over the educational process. One veteran educator summarized the state of his occupational wellbeing by noting, "When I started teaching in the 1970s, I was a teacher in the classroom. Now, in the classroom, I am a father, a youth pastor, a cop, a social worker, a friend, and, for about twenty minutes a day, a teacher."

It's no wonder that maintaining occupational wellbeing as a teacher is a challenge.

Occupational Wellbeing: The Keys

Key #1: Develop Effective Professional Community

Consider the following list of behavioral concerns I've collected in my work with K-12 schools:

- *They don't know how to manage their emotions.*
- *I am so tired of all the jealousy, drama, and nonsense.*
- *They are always up in everyone else's business and talk about other people all of the time.*

- *If someone does something good, others only try to tear them down.*

- *They are incredibly immature.*

- *It's like they feel they have permission that since they've done their time in school, now they can be mean, sarcastic, and rude.*

- *The school was a den of gossip, even after gossiping and tattling was addressed and discouraged.*

- *I see so much back stabbing.*

Ready for the kicker? These comments came from teachers who were describing not their students, but the relationships among teachers on their campuses. Ouch. When this level of mistrust exists at any level—grade, campus, or district—finding occupational wellbeing can be extremely difficult.

Julie Kochanek is a researcher with the Department of Sociology at Southern Oregon University who is known for her research in the area of relational dynamics in schools. In her book *Building Trust for Better Schools*, Kochanek notes that while trust is necessary on many relational levels (e.g., among teachers, among teachers and administrators, among teachers and parents, among teachers and students), the starting point is establishing trust among teachers and between teachers and administrators. When trust at this relational level has been eroded by toxic interaction, the repair to campus culture can take years. Kochanek observes that trust building is

> "a developmental process in which each party comes to understand what is necessary to sustain the other's trust through the development of a collective identity or the creating of joint goals and shared values."

One veteran teacher put it this way:

> "I think of my team as my spouse. Sometimes we get along, sometimes we don't. The idea is to remain professional and keep the kids in mind.

We've definitely had squabbles, and some people have difficult personalities. I'd venture to say there are fewer people more difficult to work with than one of my team members, but we have the mentality that she has a lot we can learn from and we'll try to kill her with kindness until she comes around. I live my life at school with these words in mind: 'baby steps.' Again, it all depends on the team!"

What I appreciate about this teacher's perspective is that she is looking at the big picture, understanding and engaging her professional relationships as long-term commitments. She is also approaching her relationships with an element of humility, looking to learn, even from a colleague who makes interpersonal interaction less than a pleasure. That approach clearly illustrates the challenge of the high road, but in the end, that perspective will foster the kind of relational environment that benefits both teachers and students.

Key #2: Set and Maintain Good Boundaries Between Work and Home

Creating and maintaining healthy, supportive professional relationships is critical to occupational wellbeing, but what happens when we leave the campus? Typically, we leave school, but school doesn't leave us. Tangibly, there is homework to grade, paperwork to complete, and grades to assign, among many other responsibilities. Intangibly, there are the conflicts and frustrations that are so hard to let go of. Between the tangible and intangible, it may seem that work never stops.

Overwork definitely is not an American phenomenon. According to a 2011 study conducted by the Organization for Economic Cooperation and Development, the Japanese and Koreans work the most minutes per day (it's not surprising, then, to know that the Japanese have created a word—*karoshi*—that means "death from overwork"). When we factor in unpaid work such as grocery shopping and housework, Mexicans and Japanese have the longest workday, followed by Canadians and

Portuguese. When both paid and non-paid working hours are factored, Americans ranked ninth.

While we Americans may not work the longest hours, we still face a crisis of negative effects, largely because we have failed to pair our work with wellness. Jody Heyman, founder of the Harvard-based Project on Global Working Families and director of McGill's Institute for Health and Social Policy, noted that, "More countries are providing the workplace protections that millions of Americans can only dream of. The U.S. has been a proud leader in adopting laws that provide for equal opportunity in the workplace, but our work/family protections are among the worst."

How do teachers' hours compare to those of other American professionals? Rachel Krantz-Kent, an economist with the Bureau of Labor and Statistics issued the following analysis of the 2008 data:

- Teachers were more likely than other professionals to do some work at home.

- Teachers were more likely than other professionals to work on a Sunday.

- Teachers were more likely than other professionals to hold more than one job simultaneously.

Time management coach and certified teacher, Tim Wilson, firmly believes in a teacher's ability to set and maintain boundaries. He divides his tasks into one of four categories:

- *What you have to do.* These are the activities that sustain your basic functioning, such as eating and sleeping. Even the time and effort you put into these essential activities is largely your decision.

- *What you choose to do.* This consists of the work you're prepared to do to maintain or achieve your desired standard of living. This category is essentially what you do to earn income.

- *What you want to do.* Anything you do, whether it's planned or not, that you would call enjoying the fruits of your labor. Recreation, past-times, hobbies, and maintaining relationships with family and friends.

- *Throw-away time.* This is the time that's wasted on activities that, on reflection, you could have stopped, rejected, ignored, or outsourced. We can't ever entirely eliminate throw-away time, but if we're deliberate, throw-away time can be significantly reduced.

By paying attention to the how, when, where, and why of time management, a teacher is able to create the space needed to begin to build a healthy margin that contributes to personal wellness.

Conclusion

Our blogging teacher Jennifer hasn't always resented teaching, but now she is professionally isolated. Her isolation makes it difficult to find the support she needs with classroom management and adapting her lesson plans to the needs of English Language Learners. These gaps in her experience and resources are increasing her anxiety and making her work much harder—though not necessarily much smarter—to accomplish a minimal amount of work. Since she is not able to manage her tasks efficiently on campus, she is forced to bring excessive work home and stay up late to get it done.

If you've been teaching for more than a week or so, I suspect you can relate, even if the details of your circumstances are different. Most teachers I know who have begun to dislike their vocation are experiencing deficits in both of the key areas outlined above. Neither deficit is insurmountable.

Certainly you have limited control over who your colleagues will be, but what you can control is how you respond to them. Adjusting the relational dynamics with fellow teachers and administrators likely will require some risk on your part—risk of being rejected, hurt, or ignored. Our tendency to flee those risks seems like self-preservation, but more often it guarantees us an isolated, unhealthy existence at work.

I can hear the response already (because I've heard it many times before and know it is true): "But Adam, you don't know who I have to work with!" No, I don't, but I do know that distrust and isolation never lead to occupational wellbeing. Start small, be patient, and be forgiving, believing that the reward of finding some healthy human interaction at work is worth the risk.

You do control what you choose to do and what you want to do, regardless of how long ago it was that you last felt in control of those categories. Rather than allowing your work to dominate your life, believe that there is a more balanced way to manage your time that will not get you fired or cost your students too much and will allow you to feel like a human again.

Summary

- Healthy, supportive relationships in the workplace are essential to occupational wellbeing.

- Setting appropriate boundaries between work and personal responsibilities is essential to occupational wellbeing.

Occupational Wellbeing: Recommendations for Action

Do:

1. Reach out to a colleague that you sense is struggling. Even if you don't have helpful advice, you can have a listening ear. Many times just being a good listener is more helpful to someone than offering them unsolicited advice.

2. Attend a training or professional development at the campus, district, or Educational Service Center level to sharpen your skill set. After the training, review the content with your colleagues, letting them know you are available to be a resource to them in that area if needed.

3. Clear the air with a colleague, parent, or student with whom you've had conflict. Be a humble listener, and seek to listen and understand them before seeking to be heard and understood. Be willing to own your part of a conflict or misunderstanding (use "I statements," such as "I feel _ about _____ because ____.") The point of the conversation is not to assign blame, but to restore mutual trust and understanding.

4. Congratulate a colleague, parent, or student for any job—big or small—that was well done. Make a habit of finding what is working on your campus and among your colleagues and do your best to call everyone's attention to it. Never underestimate the value of an encouraging e-mail, comment, or gesture.

5. Practice utilizing your colleagues as a resource. Schedule a conference with a colleague experienced in your content area to gain ideas about instructional strategies or classroom management ideas. Ask your campus or district-level administrator to connect you with a district behavior management or curriculum specialist.

6. Discuss your morning and evening schedule with your spouse, children, or roommate to create boundaries that will allow you to disengage from work—even if for twenty minutes—when you are home. Let them know you have a need to create space and time separate from your work, and ask them to partner with and help you be successful. Let them know specifically and individually what they can do to help, and let them know specifically and individually how they will benefit from the change.

7. Watch Brené Brown's TED talk: The Power of Vulnerability. This video absolutely is worth twenty minutes of your time. http://www.ted.com/talks/brene_brown_on_vulnerability.html

8. This Saturday night, watch *The Dead Poets Society*; *The Man Without A Face*; *The Prime of Miss Jean Brodie*; *Mr. Holland's Opus*; *Up the Down Staircase*; *To Sir, With Love*; *Music of the Heart*; or *Stand and Deliver.*

Don't:

1. Ignore or avoid colleagues, students, or parents with whom you have had conflict or pretend that no conflict occurred.

2. Ignore your feelings.

3. Attack, blame, or criticize a colleague, student, or parent in attempting to resolve conflict.

4. Vent your frustrations with one colleague, student, or parent by gossiping about them to another.

Mr. Parker's Power to Change Joey McGee's Life

The course of my life was significantly altered because of people who took the time to pause in their lives, call me to attention, and subsequently speak into mine. Mr. Parker—an 11th grade instructor at John F. Kennedy Senior High in New Orleans, Louisiana—was one of those persons. Who I am today notably bears the mark his influence.

"Mr. McGee, sit down—I want to talk to you!" he demanded, as I meandered into his classroom one afternoon early after lunch. "I just want to know one thing: why are you so sycophant?" he questioned. "Sick of what?" I responded, as the heaviness of his confrontational tone wrapped itself around my mind. "Sy-co-phant!" he repeated as he thrust a dictionary in front of me. After a few moments I found it:

Sycophant: A self-seeking, servile flatterer.

Ughh—I was busted and exposed: servile flatterer; brown-noser; a suck-up. All semblance of any facade I upheld lay shattered on the floor at his feet. In my junior year of high school, I was an overweight, insecure, and needy kid who would do just about anything to fit in. I wanted to belong. With the poignancy and wisdom of a prophetic sage, Mr. Parker spoke into my life that afternoon and challenged my self-perception: difference was not something to be despised. Rather, it was something to delight in. He further encouraged me to press into my own uniqueness, to value those propensities he pointed out in me—insightfulness, intelligence. I was outstanding—not an outcast.

I don't know what prompted Mr. Parker to confront me that afternoon. Perhaps he was seeing the unhealthy thing in me that he had wrestled with himself at one time. That afternoon confrontation lasted, maybe, twenty minutes. But its impact still resonates with who I am today and is a rudder guiding me in who I am continually becoming. Today, as a full-time musician, I know that I am an artist, and that my life was destined to be different from many of my peers.

Thank you, Mr. Parker, for teaching me to accept and embrace myself.

Joey McGee

Singer/Songwriter

Questions for Discussion

1. Would you rather have an assistant to do all your paperwork or an assistant to interact with all the parents of your students?

   I'm answering this in my role as a psychologist. Let's see... how can I put this? Dealing with paperwork is not one, but three thorns in my flesh. Let the assistant take the paperwork, and I'll take the parents, any day.

2. Which educators have been role models to you throughout your career?

   Polly McRoberts, Sharon Brewer Stahli, and JoElla Exley. They were my English teachers in 9th, 10th, and 12th grades, respectively. Every student in their class knew two things: the first was that they truly cared about us, and the second was that they weren't going to put up with any of our nonsense. When I failed out of college after my freshman year, I eventually went back to college several years later, taking one or two courses at a time, and I majored in English. At the time, I was doubtful I would ever graduate, but I figured studying English was my best hope, because these three teachers had always affirmed my writing ability.

3. What three things would you change about your particular role as an educator?

   In my role as a psychologist, I would change having to deal with insurance companies (in Chapter 1 I asked you not to get me started... are you trying to get me started again?). I would increase the level of collaboration among schools, pediatricians, and outpatient providers.

4. How satisfied are you with the level of community you experience on your campus?

   I am moderately satisfied with my level of professional community in my practice. I work with five other clinicians, all of whom are exceptionally skilled at what they do professionally, and lots of fun to be with personally. The only challenge is that since we set our own schedules, there's a lot of hit and miss. Sometimes I wish for more consistent, predictable times for everyone to be together.

5. Who is one person you could attempt to build a healthier relationship with on your campus?

    In my practice, I tend to focus on maintaining healthy and frequent interaction with the office manager and the support staff. They hold the place together, and I want to be particularly mindful of their needs and concerns.

6. What part of your home life takes the biggest hit when you bring work home?

    Quality time with the kids, definitely. Our girls are twelve and eleven, and our boys are ten and eight. We usually manage to make it to the kids' events—sporting, music, youth group, etc.—but when I'm working too much, we lose the quality down time of just hanging out at home, being together, laughing and having fun.

"Researchers have found that even more than IQ, your emotional awareness and abilities to handle feelings will determine your success and happiness in all walks of life, including family relationships."

~John Gottman, in

Raising an Emotionally-Intelligent Child

CHAPTER 4

Emotional Wellbeing

"Every time I look at my lesson plans, I feel panic—my heart races and I can feel my body getting tense. When it's really bad, I get these headaches that last for two days…. Call me crazy, but sometimes I honestly don't know who I can trust and who I can't on this campus—maybe I've just been stabbed in the back one too many times."

The teacher who is not experiencing emotional wellbeing typically struggles with feeling paralyzed by difficult circumstances and/or moods that are either avoided or poorly controlled. This emotional turmoil also tends to contribute to unhealthy interpersonal interactions in both personal and professional settings. If I am that teacher, I am experiencing a life that seems stifled, unfulfilled, and unfair. And, as much as I don't want to acknowledge it, I probably am, at some level, an emotional drain on those who depend on me.

Are you that teacher? If so, your hope lies in the reality that you have power to truly experience and express the complete, normal range of emotions in ways that are healthy and life-giving both to you and those around you. You also have power to release yourself from the emotionally toxic wells of unforgiveness and resentment that steal joy from your life on a daily basis.

What is Emotional Wellbeing?

Defining emotional wellbeing isn't quite as straightforward as defining physical wellbeing, which can be quantified in measurable terms like weight and activity. Generally, though, emotional wellbeing can be thought of as the degree to which we are able to appropriately experience and express the wide range of emotions that are part of the human experience.

This is a component of our overall wellbeing most of us are prone to neglect. We often mistake the lack of any overt psychological symptoms for emotional health. But is that really wellness? Are we satisfied to simply not be a wreck? Though it may require some work and, at times, painful self-assessment, working toward emotional wellbeing is crucial to your contentment and success, both as a teacher and as a human being.

Emotional Wellbeing: The Keys

Key #1: Appropriately Experience and Express Emotion

Emotions are often categorized as either positive (e.g., happy, enthusiastic, confident) or negative (e.g., angry, frustrated, anxious). I try to avoid parking emotions in either category, because any emotion can be positive or negative, depending on how we understand it in a given context. As we consider our ability to experience and express emotion, it may be more helpful to think of emotions as "comfortable" or "uncomfortable." Comfortable emotions, generally, are those that we feel most capable of experiencing and expressing, and uncomfortable emotions are those that we feel least capable of experiencing and expressing.

Our English word "emotion" comes from a Latin root meaning "to move." We can think of any emotion as a fuel source. When I refer to *experiencing* an emotion, I'm referring to the act of allowing the fuel into the emotional fuel tank simply by acknowledging its presence; when I refer to *expressing* an emotion, I am referring to the act of converting the emotional fuel into an action.

Much of how we understand emotion is rooted in our childhood experience. Believe it or not, that's not just a stereotype for sitcom psychologists. It's true. In an ideal situation, parents or primary caregivers are continually modeling, a) that all emotions are acceptable—though not always necessarily pleasant—for *experience*; and b) that all emotions can be *expressed* in ways that contribute to the emotional wellbeing of all individuals in the family.

As those of us who have children will attest, though, that ideal situation doesn't always play out in practice, even in the healthiest of families. Our day-to-day lives are prone to communicate spoken and unspoken rules about which emotions are acceptable and unacceptable for experience, and we run the risk of expressing emotions with words and actions that can be harmful to those around us.

In *The Different Drum: Community Making and Peace,* American psychiatrist, M. Scott Peck, eloquently describes the emotional environment in his family-of-origin:

> "Each of my parents was responsible and caring. There was plenty of warmth, affection, laughter, and celebration. The only problem was that certain emotions were unacceptable. My parents had no difficulty being angry...[but] never once one in all my years of growing up did I ever hear either of my parents say that they were anxious or worried or scared or depressed or anything to indicate that they felt other than on top of things and in total control of their lives... the problem is that I was not free to be me."

Peck would go on to experience debilitating anxiety and depression as a young adult because experiencing and appropriately expressing those emotions were not modeled for him in childhood.

Did you grow up in a family in which a certain emotion was not permitted (anger, for example)? Or, maybe experiencing anger was permitted, but it was expressed in a way that was damaging to members of the family, perhaps through verbal or physical aggression.

If so, you likely did not learn as a child to appropriately experience and express anger as an adult. You probably learned long ago to talk yourself out of feeling angry, and now you no longer are able to recognize it when it knocks. You probably learned to focus on verbal and behavioral feedback that convinces you that you are doing the right thing by avoiding anger: "You are such a laid back person. I've never seen you get angry. I love that about you." This pattern only reinforces the limitation. This same unhealthy pattern can develop around any emotion that makes us feel uncomfortable (even happiness).

Yes, there can be immediate benefits to stifling emotions. Again, emotions are fuel, and avoiding emotions, in the short term, relieves us of the psychological work of having to acknowledge and express them. But what long-term risks are we running? As we avoid emotion, we lose the authenticity of our human experience. Practically, that loss of authenticity translates into less effective relational interaction between you and your students, you and your colleagues, and you and your family and friends.

Key #2: Practice Requesting and Extending Forgiveness

When we are wronged, our instinctive response is to seek retaliation. Italian psychiatrist Roberto Assagioli aptly noted that "without forgiveness, life is governed by an endless cycle of resentment and retaliation." The endless cycle Dr. Assagioli is referring to here has also been called a "life trap" by psychologists Jeffery Young and Janet Klosko. In their book Reinventing Your Life, Young and Klosko present the powerful clinical cases of individuals who have become stuck in life due to issues of unforgiveness. Essentially, until we find resolution and healing through forgiveness in relationships, even when we escape those particular relationships through divorce, ended friendships, the death of the other person, etc., we are prone to recreate them in an attempt to find resolution and freedom. A classic example of a life pattern playing out can be found in the individual who repeatedly ends up in destructive romantic relationships. The key to healing is not found in compensating for one broken relationship with another, but in true forgiveness.

Our relational patterns often offer us evidence that we need to forgive, particularly when we find ourselves engaged in relational patterns in which themes emerge. Fear of being abandoned, fear of being taken advantage of, unhealthy dependence, unrelenting standards, entitlement and fear of healthy interdependence are all characteristics of unhealthy motives in relationship-building.

Webster's defines forgiveness this way: "to grant free pardon and to give up all claims on account of an offense or debt." I counsel my patients that forgiveness is simply surrendering the right we think we have to punish someone for the pain they've caused us. When we reach that point of surrender, we become free to engage relationally from a healthier base. In my practice, I've worked with patients who were unable to give or receive forgiveness simply because they've developed false assumptions about the nature of forgiveness. Through our sessions, as we uncovered the true nature of forgiveness, their capacity to forgive increased dramatically.

Let's examine three myths about forgiveness:

Myth #1: I can't forgive them because they won't admit to wrongdoing.

Truth: We are in complete control of our ability to forgive, and we do not need a confession of guilt from the offending party to offer forgiveness. While this situation is not ideal, it is sometimes necessary. You are not cursed to carry unforgiveness indefinitely until or unless someone else changes.

Myth #2: I must forgive and forget.

Truth: Forgetting may take years, if it happens at all. Many people make the mistake of believing that remembering the painful experience is, necessarily, evidence that forgiveness has not occurred. Not so. In reality, extending forgiveness is the first step in our healing, and as we heal, we are likely to have clear memories of the painful experience. So, I don't necessarily have to forgive *and* forget, but I almost certainly have to forgive to heal.

An analogy: let's say I'm playing basketball with someone, and they intentionally foul me and break my finger in the process. Whether they admit to wrongdoing, I am free to forgive them—to free myself from the negative emotion of unforgiveness and the lie that I have to punish them emotionally to bring justice to my broken finger. As my finger heals, though, every time I touch it, I will feel pain, and that pain will remind me of the foul. Eventually, my finger will heal, and I will be able to touch it without automatic memories of the painful foul. In fact, memories of the foul will grow less frequent. The real evidence of forgiveness, then, isn't whether I'm still remembering the foul, but whether I'm in a process of healing such that I am able to engage that person (and anyone else I meet on the court) without unnecessary anger, defensiveness, spite or vengeance.

Forgiveness is largely an intellectual decision to surrender a debt we feel we're owed; healing, on the other hand, is the sometimes long and always emotion-laden process of clearing out the powerful feelings associated with the debt. Extending forgiveness can be a relatively quick process; reaching healing, however, can take much longer.

Myth #3: If I forgive them, I'm just asking them to hurt me again.

Truth: Forgiveness does involve our surrendering a debt we feel we're owed, but it does not mean that we don't take appropriate measures to wisely steward our lives moving forward. Let's go back to the example of the foul in basketball. Again, I can forgive the other player even if they insistently deny wrongdoing or culpability. However, if I find myself unable to communicate with the other player about the foul (How did that happen? What do you consider a foul? Have you fouled before? Was I doing something I shouldn't have been doing? How can we make sure something like this doesn't happen again?), then certainly I will think twice about stepping on the court with them again. The goal in this analogy is not to play basketball with only those whom we know will not injure us, but to play basketball with those who respect us enough as a player to engage in honest dialogue when things like this come up. The key is that we don't change what we do to punish the other person or create a harbor for our own anger and unforgiveness.

While the act of forgiving can be difficult, there are numerous benefits to extending forgiveness. Katherine Piderman, Ph.D., staff chaplain at Mayo Clinic, Rochester, MN, encourages wronged individuals to "move away from your role as victim and release the control and power the offending person and situation have had in your life. As you let go of grudges, you'll no longer define your life by how you've been hurt." Researchers have linked unforgiveness with a wide range of mental and physical disorders, including depression, anxiety, eating disorders, nicotine dependence, headaches, and physical tension. Clinging to unforgiveness inevitably damages you far more than it punishes the offending party. Conversely, research has also identified several key adaptive, quality-of-life characteristics in individuals who practice forgiveness: empathy, emotional intelligence, life satisfaction, and spiritual wellbeing.

Conclusion

Jennifer is clearly lacking emotional wellness: feeling stabbed in the back and not knowing whom you can trust at work are not good building blocks for professional community. Her harboring unforgiveness hurts her in at least two ways. First, it keeps her from finding emotional healing from her past wounds, and second, it keeps her from developing healthy collegial relationships on her current campus.

Underestimating the importance of emotional wellbeing is one of the most predictably devastating choices a teacher can make. Unfortunately, it also is one of the most common, not only for teachers, but for all of us. We tell ourselves that we don't have time to deal with our emotional struggles. We resist because we know it will require us to be vulnerable. We lash out when anyone gets too close to our emotional weaknesses or wounds.

All of those responses are understandable, but the consequences of allowing them to control us are significant. We find ourselves deeply frustrated with the inappropriate expressions of those around us, yet we find ourselves resisting what we can change—our own emotional wellbeing, including and maybe especially our willingness to forgive. This, again, is good news. Your emotional health, as a person and as a teacher, is not dependent on the health of those around you. You can grow emotionally, and as you do, your capacity for forgiving and fostering meaningful relationships—with students, with other teachers, with administrators, and with your family and friends—also will grow.

Summary

- Emotion is fuel. To experience an emotion (fill the tank) is simply to acknowledge its presence. To express the emotion is to convert the fuel into action.

- "I can't" or "I must" beliefs about emotion deteriorate emotional wellness by keeping us from experiencing and expressing emotion appropriately, imprisoning us as victims of our own emotions.

- Forgiveness is critical to emotional wellness. Since we need resolution and freedom, unforgiveness of others or ourselves locks us into repetitive, maladaptive relational patterns.

Emotional Wellbeing: Recommendations for Action

Do:

1. Ask someone you trust to give you honest feedback about whether you seem to have difficulty experiencing or expressing any particular emotion. Ask them to give you examples or situations in which you have acted irrationally. Be sure to assure them that it's safe for them to be honest. Just listen and don't defend yourself. Thank them for their honesty.

2. Reflect on your family-of-origin experience: what was modeled for you as a child? Which emotions were and were not allowed, and how were the allowed emotions expressed?

3. Connect in person or by phone with someone you need to forgive. If direct contact is not practical or feasible, choose to extend forgiveness this moment, even if they cannot or will not admit to wrong-doing. Remember: surrender the right you think you have to punish them for the harm they've cause you; your forgiving means that debt is cancelled.

4. Connect in person or by phone with someone you've offended to request their forgiveness.

5. Create a time of quiet and solitude to forgive yourself for poor choices you have made in the past. After you forgive yourself, give yourself freedom not to punish yourself any further for the offense. Accept yourself warmly and be kind to yourself. Sometimes we fail to extend the grace and love to ourselves that we would extend to a friend without thought or hesitation.

6. Love yourself well by being patient as you allow yourself and relationships to heal.

7. If necessary, schedule an appointment with a counselor to explore difficulties experiencing and/or expressing emotion. (Counseling also can be very helpful in providing guidance and structure in situations in which extending or receiving forgiveness is needed).

8. Watch Brené Brown's TED talk: The Power of Vulnerability. (Yes, I already recommended this. Watch it again. It's worth it.)

   http://www.ted.com/talks/brene_brown_on_vulnerability.html

Don't:

1. Minimize the negative impact harboring unforgiveness has on your emotional wellbeing (e.g., "Whatever. It's no big deal. I'll just forget it and move on.")

2. Talk yourself out of having a tough conversation with anyone with whom you have experienced conflict.

3. Fall into the trap of allowing moments of forgiveness to become opportunities for greater conflict or deeper hurt. Whether you're seeking forgiveness or extending it, the goal is cancelled debt, not one last chance to explain yourself or focus on your pain.

Mr. Sarasin's Power to Change Tina Sabuco's Life

When I first met Mr. Sarasin, I could tell right away that he was going to be "up my alley!" He wore fun ties, purple shirts, smelled good, smiled a lot and had kind, caring eyes. He also had an uncanny ability to excite his students about whatever he was teaching, making us feel like we were a part of what was going on in the classroom and not just being "taught at."

Mr. Sarasin nurtured creativity in his students. Here's the best example: every month each homeroom had a special mass in the small chapel in our Catholic school. Mr. Sarasin would see to it that our mass was truly special. He would always choose a theme and/or ask us to help choose a theme. Then he invited us to decorate the chapel thematically! I can still picture how the chapel looked on the day we celebrated "All God's Creatures." He invited us to each bring a favorite stuffed animal and place it in front of the altar. As always, I went overboard and brought about fifteen stuffed animals. I remember him just being happy that I was excited about sharing them, instead of chastising me, as some of my former teachers might have. I love that I still can see that altar and that I still feel so special about creating that mass.

To this day, I am considered the "Theme Queen," not only in my social life (giving parties and decorating my home), but even more important, in my life's work. I created my whole company, ARTS ALIVE!, based on the notion of how the use of theme can ignite the spark in a child and excite her or him about whatever is being taught. Mr. Sarisin was instrumental in unleashing my creativity and teaching me the difference between doing paint-by-the-numbers "art" as opposed to true art. When people ask what I do, they often also ask, "How did you ever come up with that?" I simply say, "I just made it up."

Thanks, Mr. Sarasin, for encouraging me to "make stuff up!"

Tina Sabuco,
Artist

Questions for Discussion

1. Would you rather be stuck in an elevator with someone who likes to talk too much or someone who hardly talks at all?

    Definitely someone who hardly talks at all. I would just enjoy the quiet and meditate. Usually, once people find out I'm a psychologist they have sixteen questions either about their kids or their mother-in-law.

2. Look at the feelings listed at the end of the chapter. Which emotions were restricted in your childhood? Which emotions were demanded in your childhood? Which emotion is easiest for you to experience (or most comfortable)? Which emotion is most difficult for you to experience (or least comfortable)?

    Most of what I saw growing up was the use of anger as a fuel to shame and to punish. As a result, I never allowed myself to experience anger because I was afraid I would express it similarly. Anger is still probably the least comfortable emotion for me to experience and express, and only as an adult am I really learning to experience and express anger appropriately. The emotion that is most comfortable for me (drawing from the list at the end of the chapter) is enthusiasm. I'm sort of a big-picture visionary type, and I love getting other people excited about good ideas. I'm not nearly as skilled with the details involved in the execution of a good idea.

3. Would you describe yourself as a forgiving person? If so, why do you suppose you are able to forgive? If not, what prevents you from being able to forgive? Do you believe reluctance or inability to forgive makes you a healthier person? Have you ever found yourself on the other end, being unforgiven by someone who felt wronged by you?

    I would not describe myself as a forgiving person. I forgive when it's necessary, but (unfortunately), that's usually only after I'm convinced that forgiveness is the only option (versus just trying to forget it and act like nothing ever happened or retaliate via severe tar-and-feather). Some of that is probably linked to my difficulty experiencing and expressing anger.

When I was working on my master's degree, I worked as a case manager for a foster placement agency. A coworker falsely accused me of sharing personal information with our boss (she said she had word-of-mouth evidence—gossip). I denied it, but she didn't believe me, and there was a pretty big rift in our working relationship. After about a week, I asked her to forgive me. She said she did, but our interaction was never the same after that.

4. How might not being able to experience and/or express emotion impact your interaction with your students? With your colleagues?

Able	Disappointed	Happy	Pleasure
Adequate	Disgusted	Harassed	Positive
Agonize	Distracted	Hesitant	Powerful
Anger	Doubtful	Hopeful	Pressured
Annoyed	Eager	Hostile	Pride
Anxiety	Elation	Humorous	Relaxed
Anxious	Embarrassment	Ignored	Relieved
Apathy	Empathy	Impatient	Remorse
Apprehensive	Energetic	Indifferent	Revenge
Assured	Enthusiastic	Inspired	Sad
Awe	Envy	Interested	Satisfied
Bored	Exasperated	Intimidated	Scared
Burdened	Excellent	Irritated	Shocked
Capable	Excited	Isolated	Shame
Cautious	Exhausted	Jealous	Stable
Certain	Exhilarated	Joyful	Stress
Charmed	Expectant	Jumpy	Sublime
Cheerful	Fascinated	Lively	Superior
Comfortable	Fear	Lonely	Surprised
Compassion	Frustrated	Love	Suspicious
Competitive	Glad	Mad	Sympathy
Concerned	Glamorous	Magnificent	Thrilled
Confidence	Glorious	Manipulated	Tired
Confused	Good	Miserable	Uncomfortable
Contempt	Graceful	Obnoxious	Uneasy
Courageous	Grateful	Overwhelmed	Used
Delighted	Great	Panic	Wary
Depressed	Greed	Peaceful	Wasteful
Destructive	Grief	Playfulness	Weary
Determined	Guilty	Pleasant	Wishful

"Whoever said money can't buy happiness simply didn't know where to go shopping."

~Bo Derek

CHAPTER 5

Financial Wellbeing

"Today is definitely one of those days I'm pretty sure I don't get paid enough to put up with this. Even if I didn't have to put up with this, I'm still pretty sure I don't get paid enough. My credit cards are all almost maxed out, and for the past three months, I've only made the minimum payments. We've talked about taking a road trip back home for Christmas, but I don't see how we're going to be able to afford it."

The teacher who is not experiencing financial wellbeing is subject to a particular stress that has been closely linked with physical illness and marital discord. If I am that teacher, I am vulnerable to stressors that likely will damage my health and quality of life, and ultimately undermine my ability to earn an income and sustain a stable home life.

Are you that teacher? If so, your hope lies in the reality that you have power to create a personal financial structure that keeps you from wondering whether you'll be able to pay the light bill. You also have power to understand both the role money plays in your day-to-day life and the psychological factors that drive your thoughts about money and your spending habits.

What is Financial Wellbeing?

When we think of financial wellbeing, we may be prone to think of the Donald Trumps and Bill Gateses of the world. We assume the financially "well" individual is one who can spend as much money as he or she wants, never worrying about whether the next debit card purchase will be declined or if their quality of life is at risk. If that is, in fact, the definition of financial wellbeing, more than 99 percent of us are in trouble. The good news, though, is that we can enjoy financial wellbeing without being a millionaire.

To understand financial wellbeing, let me give you a preview of the definition of physical wellbeing: it is not the absence of illness, but the body's capacity to fight illness. Similarly, the definition of financial wellbeing can be thought of not so much as the absence of financial stressors (e.g., I can spend all my money on anything I want because I have no debt and exceptional surplus), but as the individual's ability to absorb financial stressors. That means that when unexpected expenses arise, such as vehicle and home repairs, medical bills, etc., I have a financial reserve to address those needs without incurring debt. Just as nurturing physical wellness requires proactive discipline over the course of time (more on that in Chapter 7), nurturing financial wellbeing requires proactive money management and disciplined attention to detail over the course of time.

Financial Wellbeing: The Keys

Key #1: Identify External Factors That Impact Your Finances

External factors in financial wellbeing refer to the nuts-and-bolts, tangible aspects of money management. In my review of personal finance resources, I've found most experts agree on the importance of the following factors:

- *Live beneath your means.* This starts with a monthly budget that outlines all of your sources of income and all of your monthly expenses. It's pretty easy for most of us to summarize the sources of our monthly income: our paycheck. For some, though, this might also include income from rental property, dividends, royalties, and other sources of passive income. Summarizing our monthly expenses isn't usually quite as easy. If we're going to be effective, including a detailed list of expenses is critical. Common categories include retirement/

savings, rent/mortgage, food, clothing, entertainment, giving, medical/dental, and home/vehicle maintenance.

- "Living beneath your means" simply means that having created a comprehensive list of your income and your expenses, your income totals more than your expenses. Many experts advocate for an envelope method, in which you have an envelope for each expense category, allocate the cash at the beginning of the month, and when the cash in a given envelope is gone, the spending in that category stops.

- *Pay off your credit cards.* There are several strategies to reduce credit card debt.

  - Transfer multiple card balances onto a single, low interest card.

  - Pay off the balance with the highest annual percentage rate first.

  - Pay off the card with the lowest balance first, while making minimum payments on the other cards. Then, move on to the next card, making bigger payments.

  - Stop using your credit card.

- *Build an emergency fund.* Experts vary in their recommendations of how big the emergency fund should be. Some recommend a fund big enough to cover a full six months of living expenses, other recommend only several thousand dollars to cover emergency medical expenses or house/car maintenance. Regardless of the size of the emergency fund, the point is to have a cash reserve that will free you from having to turn to credit cards in emergency situations.

- *Seek wise counsel.* Counsel can come in a variety of forms, including face-to-face consultation with a financial planner, online resources, or books. If your budget permits, you are wise to invest in hiring a certified financial planner to help you establish and maintain short and long term goals for financial wellness. If your current budget does not permit that expense, though, many resources are available for free online or at the public library. You also probably know someone with experience and skills in managing money. Don't be too proud to ask for help.

- *Review progress*. For most of us, our income is consistent and our expenses vary. Since we are faced with this level of unpredictability, once we've established a monthly budget, it is important for us to come back and review on a quarterly basis. Have we left any category out of our budget? Have we under or over-allocated in any category?

Coming to grips with the external factors that impact your finances is mostly a matter of putting pencil to paper and crunching numbers. The problem most individuals have in the process is failing to take into account obscure or hidden expenses, so it is wise to find a pre-set budget guide with extensive line items for each category. Use Google—you'll find dozens of websites with free excel spreadsheet downloads.

Key #2: Identify Internal Factors That Impact Your Finances

Reviewing the external factors that impact finances is the fairly straightforward process of looking at numbers and doing math. Investigating the internal factors that impact finances, however, can be a more ambiguous task. Many money-management experts agree that the state of our financial wellbeing can simply be a symptom of our psychological/emotional wellbeing. The following factors are critical in shaping our relationship with money.

- *Family of origin standard of living*. If my salary as an adult does not happen to fall in the same range as my parents' (e.g., my dad was an investment banker and I am a teacher), I may need to rethink the standard of living that makes sense on my income. Young professionals who are quick to recreate the material feel of life—housing, transportation, clothing, entertainment—they enjoyed as children may be setting themselves up for significant financial stress if their current income cannot support those expenses.

- *Family of origin attitudes.* What instruction did I receive, if any, from my parents about money? Did my parents teach me to delay my sense of gratification by saving money to purchase, or did they buy me what I wanted, when I wanted it, using their credit card? Did my parents convey beliefs—accurate or inaccurate—about money (*"Money is the root of all evil, so if you have money, you must be evil." "Don't trust banks or anyone else to tell you what to do with your money." "Money is just a tool. Treat it as such."*). How is either the lack of instruction or the presence of poor instruction currently impacting how I relate with money? What deep-seated beliefs do I have about money now that I know are inaccurate and need to be replaced?

- *Personal history with money.* Apart from what was modeled for us, our own early behavior with money can shape our current financial behavior. How did we feel when we had our own money? Guilty? Powerful? Afraid? If our early experiences managing money independently were tainted with difficult feelings and we have never talked through or processed those experiences, we may be demonstrating financial irresponsibility as adults that are rooted in those early financial experiences.

- *Money as medication.* When we use money to change how we feel, money becomes like medication. Of course, there is a time and place for medication, but any doctor will tell you that two critical issues to consider in pharmacologic treatment are tolerance and dependence. Tolerance refers to our body's propensity over time to need more of the same medication to experience the same result. Dependence refers to our body's eventual inability to function properly without medication. When we use money like medication, not only will we need bigger purchases to make us feel better (tolerance), but we will also come to a point at which we can't feel good unless we are spending money (dependence).

Accessing an outside, objective perspective is both essential and potentially difficult, as it requires us to have the humility to be transparent with someone else about what we're doing with our money. In my practice, I've worked with many couples and individuals who were experiencing significant financial stress but were at a standstill because fear and pride kept them from surrendering enough to asking for financial support and accountability.

Conclusion

Jennifer's financial wellbeing is limited. Credit card debt and emotional spending have created a financial hole that is making any hope of relief seem like a distant fantasy. Truthfully, even if she were offered a considerable raise, her spending habits would most likely place her back in a position of debt in a matter of time.

Like many of our other categories of wellbeing, financial challenges often make us feel trapped. However, unlike our other categories, this one often feels completely out of our control. No matter how much we want to be financially healthy, we can't plant a money tree and make everything well. Teachers often feel especially handcuffed by modest salaries and long hours that prevent them from pursuing other sources of income.

The truth is that financial wellbeing takes time, but once again, the point is to focus on what you can control. Organizing your external factors and bringing awareness and discipline to your internal factors will allow you to take positive steps toward a healthier financial lifestyle. Even if you only tackle one piece of the process at a time, keep moving forward. Remember, the goal is to order your life in healthier ways so you are able to better cope with the inevitable financial stresses all teachers will face.

As that happens, you will discover a new freedom to teach without excessive anxiety about whether teaching will be the source of your financial ruin. You already know you aren't teaching to get rich. Now, you'll know you aren't teaching to go bankrupt.

Summary

- Financial wellbeing isn't directly about how much money we have; some millionaires are financially unhealthy, and any teacher can be financially healthy with planning and discipline.

- External factors that impact our financial wellbeing include living beneath our means, seeking counsel, and continually reviewing our progress.

- Internal factors that impact our financial wellbeing include what was modeled and taught in our family of origin, our personal history, and relationship with money and using money as medication.

Financial Wellbeing: Recommendations for Action

Do:

1. Establish accountability, and reward yourself for your self-discipline.

2. Educate yourself about money-management basics either through books, video, or other media.

3. Consult with a financial planner to assess your income and expenses and to create a monthly budget.

4. Reflect on your family-of-origin experiences with money and discuss those experiences with someone you trust to determine how your beliefs about money might be distorted or inaccurate.

5. Have two conversations about finances: one with someone who makes substantially more money than you and one

with someone who makes substantially less money than you. Allow those conversations to shape how you define and categorize your current wants and your current needs.

6. Think back to your spending habits and lifestyle when you made less money than you do now (maybe as far back as college). Allow the contrast to shape how you define and categorize your current wants and your current needs.

7. Practice regularly giving away some percentage of your income to a nonprofit agency of your choice or to someone in need.

8. Watch an episode of *Hoarders* on Netflix. This series will give you a deeper look into the psychology of our attachment to material possessions.

Don't:

1. Equate material wealth with personal worth. One is a function of how much "stuff" you can accumulate. The other is about determining your real values and investing your money and life accordingly.

2. Believe that your financial situation is hopeless. You may have your work cut out for you as you shore-up your financial wellbeing, but all things are possible.

3. Let your pride prevent you from getting the help you need. Money is one of the final frontiers of vulnerability and community, and most of us keep this part of our lives as private as possible. Sadly, we often cut ourselves off from freedom that is within reach because we simply will not let go of the need to maintain appearances.

Ms. Wilson's Power to Change Dennis Welch's Life

When I was in high school I knew everything. I grew up in the deep south, and I was raised by people who were going through the growing pains of learning about equality, fairness, and prejudice. My education about prejudice and fairness began abruptly in the fall of 1973, when my civics teacher suddenly stopped showing up for class. We had substitutes of all shapes and sizes for a week or two. Then, one day, Ms. Wilson, our new full-time teacher, walked into our class and literally changed my life in just twenty-four short hours. She said hello and introduced herself, and then said "Boys and girls, this is Black History Month. So, we are going to study black history. Everybody ok with that?" Because I knew everything, I felt obligated to comment. I raised my hand and blurted out "well, if this is Black History Month, when are we gonna have White History Month?"

What happened next is a bit of a blur, but I have a general idea, and it goes something like this: Ms. Wilson walked me outside the class into the hallway, and this very articulate, brilliant, proud black woman proceeded to dress me down verbally until I felt about a foot tall. It turned out that along with being all of the above, she was also a trained lawyer, and her training worked very well. She methodically laid out her case for why I was a bigot and then she did me the biggest favor any teacher has ever done for me: she forbade me from coming back onto her classroom. She sent me down to the library to check out a few specific books on racism and prejudice, and she told me that the only way I could come back into her class was if I would deliver an oral report on why Black History Month mattered, and why we were celebrating it.

The next day, I stood up in front of a room full of my smart-aleck and equally bigoted classmates and told them why we were wrong to think like a bunch of small-town white supremacists. I must have done a really fine job on my presentation, because afterwards Ms. Wilson sat me down and asked me what I planned to do with my life. I planned to be a machinist like my dad, but she suggested other plans. Over the next year, I met with Ms. Wilson often to discuss my future, and she inspired me to earn an undergraduate degree and an MBA from the University of Houston.

I lost touch with her after high school, but if I could see her again I would tell her that whatever else she has accomplished in this life, she made a huge difference in mine, and I am eternally grateful. Thank you, Ms. Wilson, for teaching me to live beyond my limitations.

Dennis Welch
Media Consultant

Questions for Discussion

1. If you could spend a $500 gift card in one store on one person other than yourself, what would you get and for whom? Why?

   I had this conversation with my kids once. I told them I would go to Wal-Mart and buy them all a year's supply of underwear. Honestly, I think I would get a gift card to Pottery Barn and give it to my wife.

2. If you could spend $500 on yourself in one store, which store would you choose?

   This is sort of a tough call. It would either be Academy or Guitar Center. At Academy, I could really splurge and buy a high-dollar fishing reel or a nice rifle for hunting, and still have enough left over for a good pair of running shoes. At Guitar Center, I wouldn't be able to get anything really trophy. I already have three sweet guitars, and I would need a lot more than $500 to get the fourth one I would want. I could, though, use the money to buy new studio recording equipment. At this point, I'm leaning toward Academy.

3. What did you learn (for better and worse) about managing money as a child/adolescent? What attitudes and beliefs did your parents convey to you about money?

   First, I learned that money is scarce. Second, I learned that people who have money must have done something wrong to get it and should not be trusted. Sadly, it's taken much of my adult life to undo that thinking, but I am so grateful to have a more reality-based understanding.

   I think the most helpful instruction I've received about money is that it is a tool, just like a hammer, a saw, or a knife. Just like any other tool, we can use it to help ourselves and others, or to hurt ourselves and others. Increased material wealth means increased power to

*help or hurt; as our material wealth increases, so does
our need for external guidance and accountability.*

4. What are your earliest experiences handling your own
    money?

    *I remember getting a job as a bag boy at a grocery store
    when I was a sophomore in high school. I took money
    out of my first paycheck and bought an album (as in vinyl
    album) by Billy Squire. It felt good. As a child, though, I
    didn't have consistent instruction about what to do with
    money.*

5. What is one area where you immediately know you can
    improve in how you manage your money?

    *I need to pay more attention to details. Our family
    operates on a budget, but I think if we were more attentive
    to details, we would realize we're doing more impulsive
    spending than we think.*

6. How does your current financial status impact your
    thoughts and feelings when you are on campus?

"Your profession is not what brings home your paycheck. Your profession is what you were put on earth to do. Do it with such passion and such intensity that it becomes spiritual in calling. "

~Virgil

CHAPTER 6

Spiritual Wellbeing

"I'm honestly thinking about switching careers… seriously, though. Why am I doing this?"

The teacher who is not experiencing spiritual wellbeing is, to reference a parable, building a life on a sandy foundation. When the storms of personal doubt and circumstantial trials inevitably roll in, that foundation tends to give way, and life becomes anything but stable (Is there a more reliable weather forecast than the one predicting those storms in the life of a teacher?). If I am that teacher, I will experience recurring gut-checks and second-guessing about whether I should be teaching—whether this never-ending fight is all there is for me in life.

Are you that teacher? If so, your hope lies in the reality that you have the power to make life choices that are consistent with your value system. You also have the power to surround yourself with individuals who share your values, encourage you, and challenge you in honest, character-building ways.

What Is Spiritual Wellbeing?

I may be wrong, but I suspect this section of the book will generate the broadest range of initial reactions from readers. The word "spiritual" is loaded with connotation, fair, or unfair. Some of you will self-identify as deeply spiritual, though what that means will vary greatly. Others will claim to not be spiritual at all, generally reacting to the assumption that to be spiritual is to be some particular brand of religion. Rather than operating from a narrow sense of spiritual health that would exclude many, I would like to reframe the term "spiritual" for the sake of our look at personal wellbeing. I believe there is a way of understanding and addressing spiritual wellbeing that is essential for everyone.

In a broad sense, spirituality is generally considered to be the uniquely human search for meaning and purpose in life. For some, that search leads to certain religious beliefs or experiences; for others it does not. In either case, the search for meaning and purpose, sometimes conscious and other times quite accidental, leads us to a particular set of values and beliefs. So when I refer to spiritual wellness, I am addressing our capacity to integrate our beliefs and values with our actions—a challenge common to all of us, no matter the particulars of those beliefs and values. And it is, indeed, a challenge.

Part of what is tricky about maintaining spiritual wellness is that, for most, establishing our beliefs and values tends to be a dynamic, life-long process that ties into a broad range of relevant issues—family, education, religion, health, wealth, community service, diversity, life experience and so on. Ongoing discussion and personal reflection are central to the process. Linking that belief and value system with our routine actions and decision-making can be an abstract process, at worst, and a tentative one at best. In other words, our spiritual development often happens *to* us before we realize it, and even when we are conscious and engaged, it is rarely a fully controlled, simple part of life. In some ways, then, maintaining spiritual wellbeing can be like the proverbial effort to nail Jell-O to a tree. I believe it is possible, though, to build a relatively simple framework for nurturing spiritual health amidst the ever-changing dynamics of life. Again, the goal is to invest appropriate time and energy in what we can control in an effort to live more fully through the circumstances of life we cannot control.

Spiritual Wellbeing: The Keys

Key #1: Link Decision-Making with Life Values

Regardless of how we *define* spirituality, the *practice* of spirituality boils down to making decisions—big and small—in the context of our value system: Should I marry this person? Should we have children? Should I choose this career? Should I try this cigarette?

Parker Palmer is an educator and founder of the Center for Courage & Renewal, which oversees the "Courage to Teach" program for K-12 educators. Palmer has written extensively in the area of teacher motivation, and he frequently reminds us of the true meaning of vocation: the word derives from the Latin *vocare*, meaning "to call." He describes the differences among a job, a career, and a calling. A job is what we might do from 9 a.m. to 5 p.m. to earn a paycheck; a career is a job with potential for advancement; a calling is what we would do if money were no object because the activity itself would be intrinsically fulfilling.

Research is consistent. Teachers who retire and, in retrospect, express enthusiasm without regret about their life's vocation (yes, they do exist) conceptualized their work not as a job, not as a career, but as a calling. Teaching from an internal sense of calling is not "I'll teach until something better comes along," but "I'm choosing this profession because my role as a teacher is consistent with my value system." At the core, the teacher who thrives in the profession places such a high premium on impacting students' lives that the inconveniences and hardships associated with functioning in an imperfect educational system cannot deter them from that calling. In essence, the call to any profession will continually ring more loudly than the discouraging "white-noise" associated with the work.

Steve Farkas, senior research fellow at the Farkas Duffet Research Group, was curious about what kept teachers consistently and deeply engaged in their roles as educators. The common denominator, he found, was that the vast majority of teachers who had sustained enthusiasm over the course of a career were those who believed they were responding to a calling in choosing the field of education. This challenged the stereotype that teachers are not satisfied in what they do.

I recognize the dilemma. Many teachers can identify some sense of calling, whether it preceded their first teaching job or emerged through real experience with students, but the purity of the calling has become muddled over time. I suspect this is more the rule than the exception in modern education. My experience in working with teachers tells me that in most cases, real hope is in the revitalization of calling, not the abandonment of it. This is why spiritual wellness—starting with a renewed connection between what really matters to you and the decisions you make about your vocation—is essential for teachers.

Key #2: Share Life with Like-minded Individuals

Just as professional community is essential to occupational wellbeing, so is personal community essential to spiritual wellbeing. Our professional community is the collection of individuals with whom we share common professional space and aspirations; our personal community is the collection of individuals with whom we share common personal values and belief about life purpose. Sometimes those two communities can overlap.

In *The Different Drum: Community-Making and Peace*, American psychiatrist M. Scott Peck outlines his observation of how community develops based on his work with hundreds of individuals participating in therapeutic encounter groups. A group arrives at community only after the individuals in the group have made commitments to quantity and quality of shared time and experience. The commitment to quantity is necessary to ensure adequate time for interaction; when a group meets only on a random or spontaneous basis, the meetings lack the frequency necessary to develop comfort and rapport. The commitment to quality is necessary to ensure that the individuals develop the mutual trust that is necessary to facilitate transparency and authenticity without the fear of rejection. In the context of a safe community, individuals are free to discuss deeply personal and emotion-laden issues, not merely for personal therapy, but as part of an effort to strengthen, refine, and integrate personal values.

If that reads more like a clinical definition than warm advocacy for community, let me try it this way: people need people. The long story of human history—whether viewed through the lens of real data or anecdotally—is that isolation and disconnection erodes our sense of being and purpose; community and meaningful interpersonal connection enhance our overall health and quality of life. Many of us have so embraced other values— perhaps most notably busyness and privacy—that we have set ourselves up to fail in areas we assume to be unrelated to those values, including a personal sense of calling and spiritual wellbeing.

If you are by nature an introvert (I am), true community is an invaluable protection against the kind of detachment that inevitably either spirals into too much/too little self-confidence or produces an aloofness that is equally toxic to one's calling. If you are by nature an extrovert, true community ensures that you live beyond surface interactions and tend to the deeper parts of your identity and calling. For all of us, meaningful, ongoing connection with others makes us human and engages our spirit so that we can invest in our calling without depending on it alone to sustain us.

Conclusion

Jennifer's question is both deep and sincere: "Why am I doing this?" It suggests that she is experiencing crisis that is not merely vocational; it is a crisis of belief and values, and it is profoundly spiritual. Her doubt extends beyond how she earns money and into her sense of calling and purpose. What she values—teaching children—suddenly feels out of sync with the career she chose. Knowing she cannot change the system in significant ways, her question is natural: *Is there any way to reconcile my values and continue this job?* And let's be honest: Jennifer needs more than platitudes about kids being "worth it." If she is going to continue to teach and find fulfillment, she needs to be able to reconnect her values with what she is doing, even if the system never changes.

I believe spiritual wellness (not to be confused with spiritual perfection) is possible, even for teachers laboring in extremely difficult environments. It won't happen overnight, but like most change, it will happen one decision at a time. Start by taking intentional steps to reconnect to your sense of purpose and calling, and then find ways to invest that energy into your daily classroom routine. Please don't try to do it alone. Relentlessly search for or build community. That won't be perfect either, but a connected crowd—even a small one—of imperfect people will change not only your perspective, but also your ability to look back at your years of teaching, not with regret, but with joy and fulfillment.

Summary

- Spirituality is not necessarily religion.
- Spiritual wellbeing is the process of effectively considering and incorporating one's beliefs and values in a decision-making process.
- Sharing life with individuals who share one's values is essential to spiritual wellness.

Spiritual Wellbeing: Recommendations for Action

Do:

1. Prioritize spending time with others who share your value system (connect with a church community or religious group; participate in community events; volunteer at a non-profit organization).

2. Evaluate (or re-evaluate) how your role as a teacher overlaps with your value system and calling.

3. Write a letter to yourself. Remind yourself why you chose to enter education, including the hopes you have for your investment in your calling.

4. Keep a "Calling Journal." Document every conversation, situation, or interaction that illustrates to you why what you do is a calling, and not just a job or a career. The point is to be deliberate and mindful when life speaks to you about the gravity of your role in the lives of your students.

5. Find a friend with whom you can press into deeper relational authenticity and transparency. We all have a built-in fear of being vulnerable, but we can grow in our ability to be less controlled by any fear. Start by asking a good question and then being a good listener. If you're met with a short response, model vulnerability by offering an honest answer to the same question.

6. Watch Mihaly Csikszentmihalyi's TED talk: Flow. This is an excellent talk on the psychological factors that constitute "a life worth living." http://www.ted.com/talks/mihaly_csikszentmihalyi_on_flow.html

Don't:

1. Practice the kind of hurried lifestyle that makes time for reflection improbable.

2. Try to live life and maintain your sense of purpose on your own. We were made for community, and our sense of who we are—a central part of our spiritual health —is deeply tied to our connections with others.

3. Believe that "this is all there is." As soon as you begin thinking that way, reject the thought and call it a lie (because it is).

Coach Criswell's Power to Change Doug Baker's Life

I learned at an early age that real men don't cry. My dad was a football coach, and I can't tell you how many times I heard him say, "Just rub some dirt in it and get back in the game." By the time I was in junior high school, I quit telling people when I was hurt and just kept things to myself. I loved movies like Scarface and Rambo, because they portrayed a "man's man," lead characters that were always in control, needed no one, and were never hindered by pain. Those men were my heroes, until a lesson in Mrs. Fallstaff's world history class changed everything.

We were studying the Vietnam War and as part of the lesson, Mrs. Fallstaff invited Coach Criswell to give a guest lecture. Most of us knew Coach Criswell as a pretty even-keel type of guy. He never seemed to get really angry, never really excited; he was pretty predictable and consistent. I don't know that any of us knew he had served in the Army during the Vietnam War. The purpose of his guest lecture was to give us an idea of the political ideas involved in the war and how those ideas influenced his role as a soldier.

The lecture started off as a fairly non-descript talk about communism and democracy and how and why the United States was invested in the events of Vietnam. As Coach Criswell continued, though, he began to talk more and more about his day-to-day role as a soldier. We noticed that at some point, his speech slowed, like he was struggling to get each word out. Then, he stopped talking, and tears filled his eyes and rolled down his cheeks.

I don't know that any of us students, in that moment, could fully appreciate the gravity of what Coach Criswell was experiencing, but Mrs. Fallstaff knew—she had told us before that she had lost seven friends in the conflict. She immediately jumped in: "Coach, thank you so much, but we can stop right here and that will be fine."

"No, no, no, Mrs. Fallstaff...I need to do this," Coach Criswell insisted, through his tears. He proceeded to describe in real terms the effects the war had and continued to have on him. He concluded by emphasizing what an honor it had been to serve his country and how he had no regrets. He thanked us for giving him the opportunity to share, and he said telling his story was part of his healing.

I was in awe. I had never seen a man model that kind of transparency, and certainly never heard that doing so was actually beneficial. Now, as a husband and a father, I always remember how necessary it is to be connected and to let people know when I'm hurting.

Thank you, Coach Criswell, for teaching me that real men understand the value of vulnerability.

Doug Baker,
Software Engineer

Questions for Discussion

1. Would you rather do something you don't like with people you like, or do something you like with people you don't like?

    Definitely something I don't like with people I do like. I love music and have played in bands before. When I've played with guys I don't like, making music just is not fun.

2. Why did you decide to become a teacher?

    Well, I obviously didn't. But as far as my current vocation, I think I've always been cut out to be a psychologist/philosopher/cleric type. Even when I was in junior high, I was deeply curious about the nature of life: Why do we do what we do? What are the internal and external factors that drive human behavior?

3. Where do you go to share life with individuals who share your values?

    I go to the members of Community Church of Bryan/ College Station.

4. When does being a teacher just feel like a job? A career? A calling?

    Being a psychologist feels like a job when I get referrals from parents who want me to "fix" their kid without being willing to do any work of their own to see what they are doing to contribute to the problem. The same dynamic can also happen in marital counseling: just "fix" my spouse without having to ask me to look in a mirror. Blegh. It also feels like a job when I spend thirty-eight minutes on the phone being looped through an automated response system trying to get an insurance company to preauthorize treatment.

Being a psychologist feels like a career when I consider the logistics of managing a clinic: there are so many services to offer—therapy, assessment, consultation to schools, etc. It seems our role as psychologists is ever-expanding.

Being a psychologist feels like a calling when I have interacted with someone else (maybe in my office, maybe on a campus) and we have both been made healthier, ultimately, by the interaction.

5. In what small ways can you reconnect your truest sense of calling as a teacher to your daily routine, even if nothing about your circumstances ever changes?

"Life expectancy would grow by leaps and bounds if green vegetables smelled as good as bacon."

~Doug Larson

CHAPTER 7

Physical Wellbeing

"I couldn't sleep last night…I could tell it was going to be an iced-peppermint-white-mocha-with-an-extra-shot-of-espresso kind of day. I know, I know—not exactly health food, but I'm finally willing to admit I've lost the battle with my weight. I'm tired of the diet roller coaster routine. By 1:30 p.m., I had my usual energy crash. You know the feeling? Like when you get to the point where you're present physically, but you have absolutely no mental or emotional energy to give. I call it 'zombie mode'."

The teacher who is not experiencing physical wellbeing is most at-risk for experiencing stress in the four other life areas (occupational, emotional, financial, and spiritual), since nutrition and sleep are our most basic life activities. If I am that teacher, I am locked in the negative feedback loop of feeling continually run-down, which in turn makes me increasingly less effective, which in turn makes me have to work harder to try to keep up, which in turn makes me feel continually run down, which… well, you get it.

Are you that teacher? If so, your hope lies in the reality that you have the power to develop, over time, eating habits that will dramatically improve how you feel and function. You also have the power to invest twenty minutes of your day into physical activities and sleep routines that will restore your energy levels and support each of the other areas of wellbeing we've covered.

What is Physical Wellbeing?

If spiritual wellbeing is the hardest to define, physical wellbeing should be the simplest. After all, we generally can measure our physical wellness in quantifiable terms. Unfortunately, we also are bombarded by 1,001 theories on what really constitutes physical health. Since our focus is on wellness, we will take the broad view I alluded to in Chapter 2.

American psychiatrist M. Scott Peck has defined physical wellbeing not as the absence of disease, but as the body's ability to fight disease. The implication: our bodies can be free of disease, but we can still be unhealthy. In fact, an estimated 65.2 percent of U.S. adults are overweight or obese, defined by having a body mass index of twenty-five or more. Thirty percent of American adults have hypertension, which tends to be a silent killer because it often goes undetected and untreated. High cholesterol is a leading contributor to heart disease, and each year, more than 500,000 Americans die of heart disease. Often these devastating diseases are preceded and caused by years of unhealthy physical conditions, neglected because of the lack of obvious illness.

Physical Wellbeing: The Keys

Key #1: Practice Healthy Nutrition

I initially titled this section "Diet," but I decided to change it after some research on the term (just look at the first three letters). No, what we're after here is not the idea of food restriction to lose weight, but food intake to promote health. Consider the following from the U.S. Health Policy Gateway website:

> "Nutrition is defined as the act or process of nourishing. The primary source of nutrition is food. The relationship that one has with food whether in relation to quantity, quality, or other factors affects greatly one's nutrition and health status."

Did you catch the word "relationship"? *Relationship!* Wait, isn't a relationship supposed to be what occurs between two people who experience ongoing, mutual emotional and intellectual interaction? Powerful insight here: we interact with food in some of the same ways we interact with people. For example, my rational mind tells me to interact with people in a way that communicates dignity and respect (the dietary equivalent of vegetables, fruits, whole-grains, and proteins), but in my irrational moments, I interact with people in a way that prioritizes my feelings and desires at the expense of their wellbeing (the dietary equivalent of my beloved Hawaiian pizza and beer).

If we are going to nourish ourselves in a healthy—or rational— way, fruits and vegetables should constitute the majority of our intake, followed by healthy sources of fat (unsaturated, as in avocados, nuts, and olive oil), and healthy proteins. Processed foods and foods with high levels of sugars and carbohydrates should be avoided. Please refer to Resource 2 at the back of the book for more detailed information about which foods fall into which categories. The resource was created from the guidelines for healthy nutrition at the government website www. choosemyplate.gov.

Remember: what's rational does not always immediately feel either good or natural. Like most steps toward wellbeing, nourishing ourselves well may require that we make some difficult choices. It may even mean giving up eating habits we have used to medicate and cope with stress. The key is to remember that the long-term payoff is real and significant. Good nutrition accounts for approximately 80 percent of our overall physical wellbeing. Whatever it costs us in immediate gratification, eating well is a true difference-maker in personal wellness.

Key #2: Exercise Regularly

Maybe you loved P.E. when you were a kid because you had a body that could tolerate P.E., but now the years have caught up and you're pretty sure you won't be earning any Presidential Physical Fitness patches this year. Erase from your mind the pictures of grueling workouts or embarrassing fitness tests. My purpose here is simply to point you toward a reasonable understanding of healthy physical activity.

There are three main areas of physical exercise: cardio, strength, and flexibility.

Cardio: Short for cardiovascular, which refers to the heart. Cardiovascular exercise raises your heart rate and keeps it elevated for a period of time. Cardio also is referred to as aerobic exercise. Examples include biking (stationary or outdoors), walking/running (on a treadmill or outdoors), aerobics and machine work, such as a stair stepper, elliptical, or rowing machines.

Strength/Resistance: We usually think of weight training when we think about building strength, but strength training can be much broader. Any exercise that focuses resistance on muscular contraction falls in this category. In addition to weight training, strength training can also be achieved using resistance bands or through body motions (e.g., push-ups, sit ups, pull ups, etc). The benefits of strength training include protecting bone health, increasing balance and body mechanics and burning calories (to keep it from being stored as fat).

Flexibility: This generally refers to range of motion around a joint and its surrounding muscle during its movement. Without targeted flexibility training, our bodies (and minds) default to rigidity as we age. Decreased flexibility means decreased range of motion, which means that our muscles will not be able to do all the good things they're supposed to do.

Practicing an exercise program that incorporates cardio, strength, and flexibility training is ideal.

Key #3: Sleep enough. Sleep well.

You've probably heard the statistic before, but most of us need eight hours of sleep each night. Some can get by on six; some need ten. Many people struggle to sleep enough or well enough to support optimum health. One of the most overlooked factors contributing to poor sleep is bedtime routine. Doctors who specialize in treating sleep disorders refer to this as our "sleep hygiene" and consider it one of the most critical factors in making sure we get enough sleep.

Two essential components of sleep hygiene are habits and environment.

Habits

- Have a fixed time to go to bed and wake up. Be consistent.
- Avoid napping, especially late in the day.
- Avoid alcohol, caffeine, and heavy/spicy/sugary foods four to six hours before sleep.
- Do not exercise right before bed.
- Have a pre-sleep routine (e.g., take a bath, read for fifteen minutes in your favorite chair, enter the bed in your favorite sleeping position).

Environment

- Use comfortable bedding, including mattress, sheets, and blankets.
- Maintain a comfortable room temperature.
- Block out visual and auditory interference (e.g., light, noise, etc.).
- Take the TV out of the bedroom. If you are using the TV to fall asleep, replace the routine with relaxation techniques such as breathing exercises or guided relaxation.

Conclusion

As you note from the excerpt at the beginning of the chapter, Jennifer is having difficulty maintaining physical wellbeing. She is offsetting sleep difficulties with excessive caffeine, which exacerbates her trouble sleeping. She is not exercising regularly or eating healthily, and both have contributed to her weight gain. The net result is that her performance at work is compromised, and she enters what she calls "zombie mode."

In my original draft of the book, this was the first area of wellness to be addressed. After reviewing the manuscript, I decided to move it to the end in hopes that I wouldn't lose half of my readers in Chapter 2 as yet another "expert" urges them to eat better, exercise, and sleep more. I know these changes often feel like the steepest of uphill climbs to many who have tried and failed to improve their physical condition. I can relate. It has taken me many years to settle into healthy patterns of nutrition, exercise, and sleep.

Let me simply offer two encouragements. The first is that I simply cannot overstate the difference making those changes has made in how I feel. I do not have a back-end deal to try to sell you a particular diet program or exercise video, so my enthusiasm is pure—eating well, exercising, and sleeping better sincerely has changed my life dramatically. If I could have somehow experienced a sneak preview of the difference, I truly believe I would have made the changes much sooner.

Finally, start simple. Focus on what you can change, even if those initial changes are small. Change one eating habit in a meaningful way. Go for a walk three times a week, and stretch before and after your walk. Stop watching TV earlier in the evening and create a short, consistent bedtime routine. Most people never make the changes necessary for physical wellness because it seems too overwhelming to change everything at once. Guess what: you don't have to change everything at once. Make one small change in each area a week for three months. Physical wellbeing is a marathon, not a sprint. Pace yourself and believe that your health is worth a few sacrifices each week. Because it is.

Summary

- Physical wellbeing is not the absence of illness, but the body's ability to effectively fight illness.

- Healthy nutrition consists of primarily fruits and vegetables, followed by healthy sources of fat (unsaturated, as in avocados, nuts, and olive oil), and healthy proteins.

- An ideal exercise program incorporates cardio, flexibility, and strength training.

- Sleeping well and enough often requires making intentional choices about your sleep routine.

Physical Wellbeing in Action

Do:

- Purchase a gym membership or workout DVD.

- Find an exercise partner and help each other stick with it.

- Consult with a nutritionist to create a daily nutrition plan. You don't always have to change absolutely everything you eat. Find a plan that will help make you take reasonable steps toward eating better.

- Practice effective sleep hygiene.

- Schedule a doctor's appointment for well-visit checkup.

- Watch the documentary *Fat, Sick, and Nearly Dead* (http://www.fatsickandnearlydead.com)

Don't:

- Be discouraged by past attempts that have fallen short. Most people fail to eat well or exercise because they've failed to east well or exercise for so many years. But thousands of people overcome that. Be one of those people.

- Believe that it's too late for you to change. It's not.
- Be intimidated by your friends who look like models or are workout freaks. Your goal is to be healthy, not measure up to anyone else.
- Eat lots of doughnuts.

Mrs. Martinez's Power to Change Maria Benavidez's Life

Mrs. Martinez changed my future with a single question: "Maria, have you finished your fafsa?"

I had no idea what Mrs. Martinez was talking about. What is a fafsa, and why would I finish one?

"My what?" I asked emphatically.

"Your financial aid form," she said. "Have you finished it?"

Financial aid form? Why would Mrs. Martinez be asking me about a financial aid form?

"No ma'am, I haven't." I responded, still not sure what she was getting at.

"Okay," she said. "Come by after school today and we'll work on it."

Mrs. Martinez was my government teacher my senior year in high school, and she was amazing. In 1978, she was the only Latina teacher in our entire high school, and I had such respect for her. I think everyone did, honestly. She carried herself with an air of confidence, yet she was always approachable and easy to talk to.

That conversation was first period, and I spend the rest of the day completely clueless about why Mrs. Martinez would ask me about a financial aid form. After school that day, I stopped by her classroom.

"College," she said. That moment in her classroom was the first time I ever even thought or talked with anyone about attending college. It was not that I made bad grades—school usually came pretty easy for me. It was just that I always assumed I would go from part-time to full-time at my job at the print shop when I graduated high school. Neither of my parents attended college, and the topic of college never came up at home. Even if I had thought about college, I knew there was no way my family could afford it. My paycheck was needed for our household income.

In the end, despite all the reasons I offered Mrs. Martinez about why college was not an option for me, she continued to persuade me, and she even made visits to my house to talk to my parents. With Mrs. Martinez's support along the way, I eventually graduated with an undergraduate degree in Industrial Distribution. Graduating college took me well over the four years it took most students, but after I did graduate, I began making enough money to save a down payment on a house for my parents. I never would have been able to do it without Mrs. Martinez guidance.

Thank you, Mrs. Martinez, for guiding me to my greatest potential.

Maria Benavides
Systems Analyst

Questions for Discussion

1. Name three things you like most when you look in the mirror.

   1) The shape of my bald head. 2) My grey hair when I'm not bald. The fact that I even have a full head of hair at this stage in the game is a minor miracle. 3) My dark skin.

2. Would you rather give up doughnuts or M&Ms for the rest of your life?

   Easy: doughnuts.

3. Name a food, meal, candy, or dessert that you associate with a nurturing relationship.

   The smell of cinnamon reminds me of the cookies my grandmother baked for my siblings and me when we stayed with her during the summer.

4. Did you play sports in high school? What is your favorite sport, and who is your favorite athlete?

   I played football in junior high, and I ran track and cross country in high school. No special awards, but I did once narrowly lose to a guy that several years later went on to the Olympic trials. I'm pretty sure he was sick the day I raced him. My favorite sport to watch is college football. My favorite sport to play is basketball. My favorite athlete is David Robinson, who played center for the San Antonio Spurs from 1989-2003. Professional athletes with the combination of his exceptional athletic ability and personal character are rare.

5. Which is harder for you: consistent healthy eating, or consistent exercise?

   I workout six days a week fairly consistently, so I would say consistent healthy eating is harder. Once I got past the first two weeks of cutting the garbage (e.g., sugar, flour, simple carbohydrates, etc.) out of my diet, the cravings decreased and my appetites began to change.

I give myself three throw-away meals a week: as much of whatever I want—fast food, pizza, whatever. If I'm not careful, though, I conveniently lose track of where I'm at in my weekly count of throw-away meals.

6. List one small change you can make in each area—nutrition, exercise, and sleep.

   Nutrition: decrease caffeine intake from two cups to one per day; exercise: doing well here, no real change needed; sleep: quit taking my laptop and iPhone into the bedroom at night!

7. Which most negatively impacts your performance on campus: poor nutrition, lack of exercise, or poor sleep?

"γν-θι σεαυτόν."

(Know thyself.)

~Ancient Greek aphorism

"We don't want to know what we really know, because if we did,

we'd have to change our lives."

Parker Palmer

CHAPTER 8

The Teacher Wellness Inventory™ and the Change Organizer™

"Is this where the sidewalk ends? Where do I go from here?

When answering the question of where to from here, I'm inclined to heed the words of American statistician W. Edwards Deming: "In God we trust; all others must bring data." Presuming that God has not yet given you a direct answer, let's look at data.

The Examined Life

You've read about wellbeing: occupational, emotional, financial, spiritual, and physical. Now it's time to take the Teacher Wellness Inventory. I created this inventory specifically for teachers based on a merge of research in the field of education, research in the respective areas assessed by the inventory, and my extensive personal experience working with teachers. It is designed to give you a visual representation of your overall wellness; in essence, you will be able to see the wheel on which your life is riding. After you complete the inventory and chart your wheel, we'll walk through Jennifer's inventory (her completed wheel is included) as a case study to give you a better understanding of how to interpret your inventory and how to organize and prioritize your changes.

How well are you? Let's find out.

Instructions

Step One: Answer True/False

Respond to the ten items in each of the five areas being assessed. Total the number of true responses at the bottom of the response page. Thus, for any given area, you will have a maximum score of 10 and a minimum score of 0.

The challenge with the True/False format is that the most honest response to some items will depend on circumstances—in some cases, your answer would be true and in other cases, false for the same question. Test-takers often hope for a 1 to 10 scale, or some other response form that gives them wiggle room. Test developers, though, know that in certain test situations, forcing the test-taker to choose in an either/or format will most effectively measure what needs to be assessed. This is one such test. Choose the answer that seems truest of you most of the time.

Step Two: Transfer Scores

After you have totaled the responses in each of the five areas, transfer those scores to the corresponding section at the bottom of the Wellness Wheel page.

Step Three: Plot Scores

Each of the five spokes represents an area: a spoke for physical, a spoke for emotional, and so on. The spoke at the center of the wheel is 0, and the spoke at the outer edge of the circle (near the rim) is 10. Place a dot or mark along each spoke according to your score. For example, if you scored a 2 on physical, you would place a mark on the spoke closer to the center of the wheel; if you scored a 9 on physical, you would place a mark on the spoke closer to the outer edge.

Step Four: Connect the Dots

As you draw lines to connect the dots, the shape of your life wheel will emerge.

<u>Occupational Wellbeing</u>

	T	F
1. I am able to let go of frustrating or challenging situations over which I know I have no control, **and** such situations do not steal from the enjoyment of my life apart from school.		
2. I am confident in my knowledge of my content areas **and** my ability to teach it to my grade level.		
3. I am generally satisfied with my vocation as an educator.		
4. I am satisfied with the relational environment and community among my colleagues on my campus.		
5. I commit energy and time to professional and self-development, both on campus and at home.		
6. I access resources (e.g., books, videos, other professionals) to improve my performance as a professional on campus.		
7. I read more than ten books a year.		
8. I am happy with the balance between my work and leisure time.		
9. I adapt to change without complaining or blaming.		
10. My time on campus is generally characterized by positive thought.		
Total Number of TRUE Responses		

<u>Emotional Wellbeing</u>

	T	F
1. I harbor no unforgiveness in past or present **personal** relationships.		
2. I harbor no unforgiveness in past or present **professional** relationships.		
3. I have a positive self-image, **and** I have forgiven myself for all my past mistakes.		
4. I have requested forgiveness and sought to make amends in all relationships in which I know I've offended someone.		
5. I seldom experience periods of depression or significant anxiety.		
6. I am able to appropriately experience **and** express anger, happiness, sadness, and fear.		
7. I stick up for myself when necessary and am not a "doormat."		
8. I do not use strong emotion such as anger or fear to injure others by speaking ill of them, criticizing them, attacking them, etc.		
9. I do not use strong emotion such as anger or fear to withdraw from my responsibilities, blame others or refuse to accept my wrongdoing.		
10. I seek help and support when I need it.		
Total Number of TRUE Responses		

Financial Wellbeing

	T	F
1. My monthly income is budgeted to account for all expenditures, and I am faithful to that budget.		
2. I am not living on a paycheck-to-paycheck basis.		
3. I am satisfied with my current financial status.		
4. I have reserve finances to cover a) an immediate $1,000 financial emergency and b) three-month's salary.		
5. I am confident about my knowledge of and ability to productively manage my income.		
6. I have less than $1,000 of outstanding consumer debt (e.g., credit cards, car loan, etc.).		
7. I am confident about being on track for a financially-successful retirement.		
8. I regularly give some percentage of my income to a cause of my choice (e.g., religious, non-profit, etc.).		
9. In the past week, I have not experienced stress about my finances in general.		
10. I have read at least five books to educate myself about how to manage my personal finances effectively.		
Total Number of TRUE Responses		

Spiritual Wellbeing

	T	F
1. I have a personal belief system (e.g., spiritual, atheist, religious, philosophical, etc.).		
2. I have a sense of belonging, meaning and purpose about my role as an educator.		
3. I am able to forgive myself and others.		
4. I participate regularly in activities with people who share my beliefs.		
5. I accept my limitations without embarrassment or apology.		
6. I practice asking trusted others about areas in my life that might need improvement or attention **and** I take necessary steps for improvement when it is needed.		
7. I freely give to others my time, money, emotional energy, and other resources.		
8. I continually explore how my personal beliefs, values, and priorities determine both my work ethic on the campus and my professional decision-making.		
9. I keep the purpose of my life clearly in mind and let it guide my decision-making.		
10. I prioritize maintaining balance among all areas of my life. (spiritual, physical, relational, emotional, and occupational).		
Total Number of TRUE Responses		

<u>Physical Wellbeing</u>

	T	F
1. I have exercised vigorously for twenty minutes for at least four of the past seven days.		
2. I eat a well-balanced and wholesome diet and follow healthy eating habits.		
3. I fall into the appropriate weight category for someone my height and sex (Use Resource 1 in the back of the book to calculate your Body Mass Index. The results probably will surprise you).		
4. I am satisfied with my current energy level.		
5. I drink less than eight ounces of caffeinated drink per day.		
6. I avoid smoking cigarettes, cigars, or a pipe.		
7. I generally get adequate and satisfying sleep, and I wake up refreshed.		
8. I follow recommended preventive health practices, such as self-examination and blood pressure checks.		
9. I am satisfied with my ability to relax without using excessive alcohol or tobacco.		
10. I am generally free from chronic or on-going illness.		
Total Number of TRUE Responses		

Interpreting Your Wheel

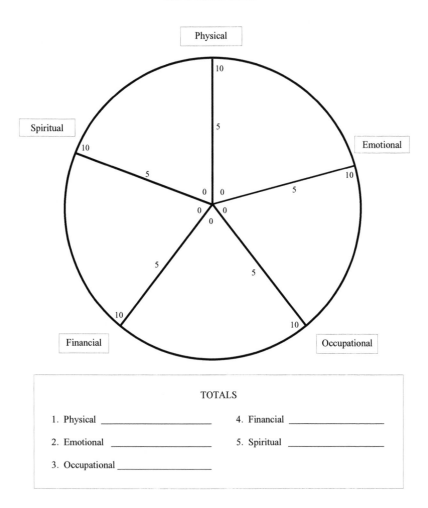

The Wellness Wheel

TOTALS

1. Physical _____   4. Financial _____

2. Emotional _____   5. Spiritual _____

3. Occupational _____

Well, how do you look?

Two key points to consider as we interpret the wheel are the wheel's size and shape. The size of our circle reflects the degree to which we are operating at our full potential. Would I rather ride on a properly inflated car tire or a flat tire? Guess which one will burn out more quickly? The shape of our circle reflects the degree to which we're living a balanced life at whatever capacity we're operating. Square-shaped wheels suggest that while we may have one or two relative strengths, there are key areas in our lives that remain under-developed. Remember from Chapter 2 that while we can be thankful for the areas in our lives in which we are experiencing wellness, those areas will, over time, begin to suffer due to weaknesses in the other areas of our lives. The four most common wheel patterns are big and circular, big and not circular; small and circular; small and not circular.

Big/Circular (BC)

These are wheels produced by scores of 8 or more in all five areas. If your wheel is big and circular, good for you! Your life is both balanced and operating at full capacity. Your life is running smoothly. Whatever you've been doing, keep doing it and continue to focus on small improvements you can make in each area!

Big/Not Circular (BNC)

These are wheels produced by scores of over 8 at least two areas, but below 5 in at least one area. You are experiencing wellness in some areas of your life. Good job! When you experience conflict and stress in your weak areas, however, your entire life will feel the bump of the stress. With enough bumps your strong points will erode in short order. The question now is when and to what degree your areas of weakness will begin to erode the progress you've made in the areas of your strengths. Your change should start with your most obvious weak area. Since your overall wheel is big, you probably have several areas of strength, so you can afford to spend more of your energy aggressively creating wellness in only a few areas.

Small/Circular (SC)

These are wheels produced when scores in each category are 7 or below and do not vary category-to-category by more than 3 points. You are living some degree of balance between categories, but you are not operating at or near full capacity. Your life may feel like it's running smoothly, but you're probably having to work much harder than is necessary to maintain that feeling. Since you don't have a pattern of obvious strengths and weaknesses, your change could start in any area. You might want to start with an area in which you feel the most intrinsic motivation. Since your overall wheel is small, you probably need to invest your energy developing wellness across several areas, so start with small, achievable goals in each area.

Small/Not Circular (SNC)

These are wheels produced by scores of up to 7 in one, two or three areas, but below 4 in one or more area. Your life feels neither efficient nor balanced. While you may show relative strengths, you are probably working much harder than you need to and not to your full capacity. When the bumps in your life hit, they will create even more difficulty for you, causing you to have to work even harder just to keep pace. Your change should start with an area of obvious weakness and build from there. Since your overall wheel is small, you potentially will be working on developing wellness in all five areas, so focus on goals that are short term and readily achievable.

Jennifer's Wellness Wheel

Let's take a look at Jennifer's completed wheel on the next page. Her relative strength is her spiritual wellbeing, in which she scored a 7. Her relative weakness is her financial wellbeing, in which she scored a 3. Based on the four wheel categories described above, her wheel falls into the Small and Not Circular category, since she has a score of up to 7 in one area (spiritual), but below 4 in one or more area (financial).

The Change Organizer

In the following pages, we'll discuss the priorities Jennifer established to address her weaknesses using the Change Organizer. But first let me better explain the Change Organizer.

The purpose of the Change Organizer is to make sure that feeling overwhelmed does not stop you from taking appropriate action and to help you create and pursue achievable goals toward health. The Change Organizer allows you to prioritize which of the five areas needs your attention first. To do this use the shaded row at the bottom of each table with the bold print "OVERALL PRIORITY (RANK 1, 2, 3, 4 or 5)."

After you establish an order for each of the five areas, you will create priorities within each given area. To do this, use the row at the right of each table with the bold print "Priority #". For example, if you rate physical wellbeing as your top priority, you can then set additional priorities within the category:

1. I am changing my nutrition;
2. I am improving my sleep habits;
3. I am exercising regularly.

Again, the hope is that the Change Organizer will move you from the panicked feeling that all is not well to a more manageable feeling that nurturing your wellness will boil down to you executing clear and prioritized tasks. Let's review Jennifer's Change Organizer to illustrate.

Jennifer chose to focus on her physical wellbeing as her first overall priority. In my work with teachers across the state, I've seen physical wellbeing most consistently lacking among the five areas. When life's demands overwhelm us, we are most likely to neglect our bodies to help us get through tough times. Unless you have a glaring weakness in one of the other four areas, this is usually a good place to start. Among the areas within her physical wellbeing, Jennifer chose nutrition first, then exercise, then weight, then sleep. A write-in area for Jennifer was to decrease caffeine intake.

(1) Physical

Physical Priority #1: I am changing my nutrition.

Physical Priority #2: I am starting an exercise routine.

Physical Priority #3: I am changing my weight.

Physical Priority #4: I am developing a healthy sleep pattern.

Other: I am decreasing caffeine intake! Ouch!

Occupational wellbeing fell second on Jennifer's list of overall priorities, and she prioritized increasing her knowledge base followed by improving professional relationships. Her sense of urgency about connecting instructionally with the English Language Learners in her class led her to first rank training in that area, followed by seeking professional development for classroom management. Her third priority was changing the nature of her professional relationship with a potential mentor teacher. Finally, she is setting boundaries to protect her personal time off campus. Her write-in goal was to be more proactive about building community with other teachers in her grade-level.

(2) Occupational

Occupational Priority #1: I am seeking a colleague for guidance on

working with English Language Learners

Occupational Priority #2: I am seeking professional development for classroom management.

Occupational Priority #3: I am changing the nature of my professional relationship with Donna. I will perceive her as a resource, and I will engage in productive conversation about classroom management.

Occupational Priority #4: I am setting boundaries to protect more of my time at home. No more missing out on key relationships so I can do schoolwork!

Other: I am reaching out to other teachers in my grade level.

Nurturing financial wellbeing fell third on Jennifer's list of overall priorities. As with her occupational wellbeing, she prioritized strategies to increase her knowledge base. It is likely that the process of increasing her knowledge base will inform how she can increase the rate of reducing her debt and how inappropriate beliefs about money might be contributing to her financial difficulties.

(3) Financial

Financial Priority #1: I am changing my knowledge about money

by taking a trip to the library to check out a book on money management.

Financial Priority #2: I am changing the rate of reducing my debt.

Financial Priority #3: I am changing my beliefs about money: money is not

evil!

Emotional wellbeing fell fourth on Jennifer's list of overall priorities. Jennifer has accepted that she continues to harbor unforgiveness toward the administrator at her previous campus, and because of that unforgiveness she is having difficulty trusting leaders at her current campus. Also, Jennifer is realizing that as a people pleaser she has never given herself permission to experience and express anger appropriately. As a result, she ends up working against herself to avoid upsetting others instead of asserting herself appropriately by setting boundaries.

(4) Emotional

Emotional Priority #1: I choose to forgive Brenda, the principal at my last

campus who was so toxic (and of whom Donna reminds me).

Emotional Priority #2: I give myself permission to appropriately experience and express anger. If needed, I will consult with a counselor for assistance in this area.

I also will read a book about how to manage my overly-passive personality.

Finally, Jennifer ranked spiritual wellbeing fifth on her list of overall priorities. Jennifer is still engaged in activities with people who share her values (although she notes that she feels the need to get more connected). She does, however, need to revisit the nature of her calling and remind herself of the clarity of purpose she had when she entered the profession.

(5) Spiritual

Spiritual Priority #1: I am spending time in quiet reflection to remind myself why I chose education.

Changes I Am Making to Nurture My Occupational Wellbeing

Occupational			Priority #
1. Do I need to change the nature of my professional relationships?	Yes	No	3
2. Do I need to set better boundaries to protect my time off campus?	Yes	No	4
3. Do I need to seek professional development in any particular area?	Yes	No	2
4. Do I need to seek out a colleague for guidance in any particular area?	Yes	No	1
5. Any other changes I would like to make to nurture my occupational wellbeing:			
OCCUPATIONAL, OVERALL PRIORITY (RANK 1, 2, 3, 4 or 5)			2

Possible Action Points to Create Change

1. I am attending training at campus, district, or Educational Service Center level.
2. I am scheduling a conference with a colleague experienced in my content area.
3. I am discussing the morning and evening schedule with my spouse/children/roommate to create the boundaries that will allow me to disengage from work when I am home.
4. Other:

Reach out to other teachers at my grade level.

Changes I Am Making to Nurture My Emotional Wellbeing

Emotional			Priority #
1. Do I need to allow myself to appropriately *experience* certain emotions?	Yes	No (circled)	
2. Do I need to change my ability to appropriately *express* certain emotions?	Yes (circled)	No	2
3. Do I need to need to forgive myself?	Yes	No (circled)	
4. Do I need to forgive anyone else?	Yes (circled)	No	1
5. Do I need to ask anyone to forgive me?	Yes	No (circled)	
6. Any other changes I would like to make to nurture my emotional wellbeing:			
EMOTIONAL, OVERALL PRIORITY (RANK 1, 2, 3, 4 or 5)			4

Possible Action Points to Facilitate Create Change

1. I am connecting in person or by phone with someone I need to forgive. If direct contact in person or phone is not practical/feasible, I am choosing to extend forgiveness this moment.
2. I am connecting in person or by phone with someone I've offended to request their forgiveness.
3. I am creating a time of quiet and solitude to forgive myself for poor choices I have made in the past.
4. I am scheduling an appointment with a counselor to explore difficulties experiencing and/or expressing emotion. (Counseling also can be very helpful in providing guidance and structure in situations in which extending or receiving forgiveness is needed.)
5. Other:

[handwritten] ★ Give myself permission to express anger appropriately.
★ Forgive colleagues who have betrayed my trust.

Changes I Am Making to Nurture My Financial Wellbeing

Financial			Priority
1. Do I need to change my monthly budget?	Yes	(No)	
2. Do I need to change the rate of reducing my debt?	(Yes)	No	
3. Do I need to change my beliefs about money?	(Yes)	No	*2* *3*
4. Do I need to change my level of knowledge about how to effectively manage money?	(Yes)	No	*1*
5. Any other changes I would like to make to nurture my financial wellbeing:			
FINANCIAL, OVERALL PRIORITY (RANK 1, 2, 3, 4 or 5)			*3*

Possible Action Points to Create Change

1. I am consulting with a financial planner to assess my income and expenses and create a monthly budget and to establish accountability.
2. I am educating myself about money-management basics either through books, video, or other media.
3. I am reflecting on my family-of-origin experiences with money and discussing those experiences with someone I trust to determine how my thinking about money might be distorted.
4. Other:

★ Trip to the library to check out a book on money management.

Changes I Am Making to Nurture My Spiritual Wellbeing

Spiritual			Priority
1. Do I need to change the amount of time I spend with others pursuing a similar value system?	Yes	No	
2. Do I need to change my decision-making processes to incorporate my value system?	Yes	No	
3. Do I need to re-evaluate my sense of purpose/calling as an educator?	Yes	No	/
4. Other changes?			
SPIRITUAL, OVERALL PRIORITY (RANK 1, 2, 3, 4 or 5)			

Possible Action Points to Create Change

1. I am prioritizing spending time with others who share my value system.
2. I am evaluating (or *re*-evaluating) how my role as a teacher overlaps with my value system and calling.
3. Other:

☀ *I need to get connected!*

Changes I Am Making to Nurture My Physical Wellbeing

Physical			Priority #
1. Do I need to change my weight?	Yes	No	3
2. Do I need to change my exercise routine?	Yes	No	2
3. Do I need to change my nutrition?	Yes	No	1
4. Do I need to change my sleep pattern?	Yes	No	4
5. Do I need to see my doctor about any physical ailment that I have been ignoring?	Yes	No	
6. Any other changes I would like to make to nurture my physical wellbeing:			
PHYSICAL, OVERALL PRIORITY (RANK 1, 2, 3, 4 or 5)			1

Possible Action Points to Facilitate Physical Change
1. I am purchasing a gym membership or workout DVD.
2. I am finding a workout partner.
3. I am consulting with a nutritionist to create a daily nutrition plan.
4. I am practicing effective sleep hygiene (see Resource 3).
5. I am scheduling a doctor's appointment for well-visit checkup.
6. Other:

Decrease caffeine intake!

Unless your wheel is big and circular, your thoughts are probably racing, and you may feel overwhelmed as you look at the areas in your life lacking wellbeing and ask, "Where do I even begin?" Before you put pen to paper to organize and prioritize your change, let me share a bit about anxiety, what it makes us do, and how we can use our anxiety to maximize our potential to actually move into the change we'd like to see in our lives.

About Anxiety

Remember, all emotion—including anxiety—is fuel. When we experience anxiety, we tend to express that emotional fuel via two behaviors: we attack (engage) or we run (disengage). You may remember learning about the flight or flight response in your Introduction to Psychology course. Both behaviors—engaging and disengaging—can be helpful or hurtful; it depends on how you choose to engage or disengage. Before we get to a point of organizing our efforts to nurture our wellness, let's review engaging and disengaging strategies—it will be important for us to keep these strategies in mind as we begin to take action.

Engaging as a Helpful Behavior

Expressing the emotional energy of anxiety by engaging is helpful when we can attack the source of our stress without harming ourselves or those around us. For example, we can use the energy to anticipate, which means connecting with someone (a colleague, friend, or counselor) who has been through our dilemma before or understands it well enough to offer us support and direction. We can also use the energy to assert ourselves appropriately, which means communicating our thoughts and feelings clearly and consistently, using "I statements" ("I feel overwhelmed at the moment, and I think I need some time to calm down" versus "This job is freaking me out and something at work has to give."). Setting clear boundaries by knowing when and how to say "no" is another example of asserting ourselves appropriately.

Engaging as a Hurtful Behavior

Not all expressions of engaging are helpful. Expressing the emotional energy of anxiety by engaging is hurtful when we harm ourselves or those around us in our attempts to alleviate our stress. For example, we might blame and attack others ("It's fill-in-the-blank's fault I'm in this mess. If he wasn't such an idiot, I wouldn't have to be dealing with this right now."). Or, we blame and attack ourselves; taking ownership of our weaknesses—and eventual wellness—is essential, but when we wallow in self-loathing, we become our own worst enemy. Strategies like these may feel good in the moment by providing a momentary release and relief, but in the long run the damage done only adds difficulty to an already problematic situation.

Disengaging as a Helpful Behavior

Expressing the emotional energy of anxiety by disengaging is helpful when we withdraw from the source of our stress to reflect and recover without harming ourselves or those around us. For example, we may tap the energy to create time to be alone for reflection and perspective. A million-dollar question I encourage my patients to ponder in times of crisis is "What might I be doing to contribute to or sustain the problem?" The point of this type of reflection is not to encourage us to beat up on ourselves, but to position ourselves to focus on the variables over which we have the most control—those within us. Time in reflective meditation can also offer perspective: how big is this problem, really? How important will this issue be in my life next week? Next month? Next year? Five years from now? By considering problems in the context of a broader time frame, we can reduce the sense of crippling urgency that often accompanies our stressors.

Disengaging as a Hurtful Behavior

As with engaging, not all expressions of disengaging are helpful, either. When disengaging takes the form of apathy, denial, or refusal to acknowledge our own wrong-doing, we run the risk of harming others by failing to maintain a necessary level of investment in a problem's resolution: "What do I care? I'm not making a difference anyway, so I'm just going to avoid the problem and act like nothing is wrong."

Maintaining an awareness of whether your expressions of anxiety are helpful or hurtful can save a lot of heartache for everyone involved as you organize the changes you need to make to nurture your wellbeing. Will you view these challenges as a mess someone else created and then fall victim to resentment? Will you view these challenges as an obstacle that cannot be overcome and retreat into denial and apathy? Or will you understand these challenges as opportunities to nurture an abundant, full life? You make the choice.

About Change

Generally speaking, we resist change. Change—even change for the better—is stressful, and we often are prone to stick with the headaches of the status quo rather than deal with the headaches of the unknown. Here are a few key points to keep in mind to maximize your likelihood for success.

First, state your goals in positive language. For example, instead of *"I will not eat junk food,"* go with *"I am eating food that nourishes my body and keeps it well."* The point here is to articulate the goal to which you are moving and not what you want to avoid.

Second, state your goal in active language. In the previous example, not only was the goal restated in positive language (*"I am eating..."* versus *"I will not eat..."*), but it was also restated in active language: *"I am eating..."* instead of *"I will eat..."* or *"I should eat...."* These may seem like irrelevant linguistic nuances, but repeated studies have concluded that our subconscious mind responds most favorably to active, affirmative statements.

Third, remember: you have time! Organizing change can be extremely helpful, but even with that, you are left with the work of change. Keep in mind, though, that this is about change that will extend into the rest of your life. It's much more about consistently practicing the new lifestyle day-to-day, week-to-week, month-to-month, and year-to-year than it is about checking things off your to-do list. In certain ways, the fact that these changes will take time works to your benefit, as it allows you to develop the discipline and routine to truly internalize your change.

Fourth, don't do this alone. Even if you could, I don't recommend it. This is a process for you to develop wellbeing as you build community. As you organize your goals, think about whom you can partner with. As you face the challenge of change, you will need support, and your community will be your biggest cheerleader. As you face the challenge of change, you will need accountability—someone to whom you must answer about keeping your commitments—and your community will be your accountability.

Finally, consider this a problem-solving process. Completing the Change Organizer is a great starting point—but it's just a starting point. By all means, make adjustments as you move forward. What is working? What is not working? Why is it not working? Which person, book, video, or other resource can I access to find good flow?

Again, keep these factors in mind as you complete the Change Organizer. Ready, set, go.

Changes I Am Making to Nurture My Occupational Wellbeing

Occupational			Priority #
Do I need to change the nature of my professional relationships?	Yes	No	
Do I need to set better boundaries to protect my time off campus?	Yes	No	
Do I need to seek professional development in any particular area?	Yes	No	
Do I need to seek out a colleague for guidance in any particular area?	Yes	No	
Any other changes I would like to make to nurture my occupational wellbeing:			
OCCUPATIONAL, OVERALL PRIORITY (RANK 1, 2, 3, 4 or 5)			

Possible Action Points to Create Change

1. I am attending training at campus, district, or Educational Service Center level.

2. I am scheduling a conference with a colleague experienced in my content area.

3. I am discussing the morning and evening schedule with my spouse/children/roommate to create the boundaries that will allow me to disengage from work when I am home.

4. Other:

Changes I Am Making to Nurture My Emotional Wellbeing

Emotional			Priority #
Do I need to allow myself to appropriately *experience* certain emotions?	Yes	No	
Do I need to change my ability to appropriately *express* certain emotions?	Yes	No	
Do I need to need to forgive myself?	Yes	No	
Do I need to forgive anyone else?	Yes	No	
Do I need to ask anyone to forgive me?	Yes	No	
Any other changes I would like to make to nurture my emotional wellbeing:			
EMOTIONAL, OVERALL PRIORITY (RANK 1, 2, 3, 4 or 5)			

Possible Action Points to Facilitate Create Change

1. I am connecting in person or by phone with someone I need to forgive. If direct contact in person or phone is not practical/feasible, I am choosing to extend forgiveness this moment.

2. I am connecting in person or by phone with someone I've offended to request their forgiveness.

3. I am creating a time of quiet and solitude to forgive myself for poor choices I have made in the past.

4. I am scheduling an appointment with a counselor to explore difficulties experiencing and/or expressing emotion. (Counseling also can be very helpful in providing guidance and structure in situations in which extending or receiving forgiveness is needed.)

5. Other:

Changes I Am Making to Nurture My Financial Wellbeing

Financial			Priority
Do I need to change my monthly budget?	Yes	No	
Do I need to change the rate of reducing my debt?	Yes	No	
Do I need to change my beliefs about money?	Yes	No	
Do I need to change my level of knowledge about how to effectively manage money?	Yes	No	
Any other changes I would like to make to nurture my financial wellbeing:			
FINANCIAL, OVERALL PRIORITY (RANK 1, 2, 3, 4 or 5)			

Possible Action Points to Create Change

1. I am consulting with a financial planner to assess my income and expenses and create a monthly budget and to establish accountability.

2. I am educating myself about money-management basics either through books, video, or other media.

3. I am reflecting on my family-of-origin experiences with money and discussing those experiences with someone I trust to determine how my thinking about money might be distorted.

4. Other:

Changes I Am Making to Nurture My Spiritual Wellbeing

Spiritual			Priority
Do I need to change the amount of time I spend with others pursuing a similar value system?	Yes	No	
Do I need to change my decision-making processes to incorporate my value system?	Yes	No	
Do I need to re-evaluate my sense of purpose/ calling as an educator?	Yes	No	
Other changes?			
SPIRITUAL, OVERALL PRIORITY (RANK 1, 2, 3, 4 or 5)			

Possible Action Points to Create Change

1. I am prioritizing spending time with others who share my value system.

2. I am evaluating (or *re*-evaluating) how my role as a teacher overlaps with my value system and calling.

3. Other:

Changes I Am Making to Nurture My Physical Wellbeing

Physical			Priority #
Do I need to change my weight?	Yes	No	
Do I need to change my exercise routine?	Yes	No	
Do I need to change my nutrition?	Yes	No	
Do I need to change my sleep pattern?	Yes	No	
Do I need to see my doctor about any physical ailment that I have been ignoring?	Yes	No	
Any other changes I would like to make to nurture my physical wellbeing:			
PHYSICAL, OVERALL PRIORITY (RANK 1, 2, 3, 4 or 5)			

Possible Action Points to Facilitate Physical Change

1. I am purchasing a gym membership or workout DVD.
2. I am finding a workout partner.
3. I am consulting with a nutritionist to create a daily nutrition plan.
4. I am practicing effective sleep hygiene (see Resource 3).
5. I am scheduling a doctor's appointment for well-visit checkup.
6. Other:

Welcome to the Rest of Your Life

Congratulations!

You've taken the Wellness Inventory and had the courage to take an honest assessment of your life. Not only that, but you've also organized and prioritized the changes that you need to make to move toward greater wellbeing. Well done!

I've said it repeatedly throughout, but let me say it again: start slow and be consistent. Any system, when faced with too much change too quickly, will go into shock. We don't want shock. We want the kind of gradual and consistent change that will produce a transformed lifestyle. If you're serious about making lifestyle changes, you'll need to discover where to land between starting out too aggressively (and burning out) and being overwhelmed with change and shutting down (rusting out).

Remember: the areas in which you are not experiencing wellness, most likely, did not become that way overnight. Just as it took time for you to drift from wellbeing, it will take time for you to purpose yourself back into wellbeing.

YOU CAN DO IT!

Now, let's check back in with Jennifer....

CHAPTER 9

The Case for Progress

unbalancedteacher.blogspot.com
March 23, 2012
9:30 p.m.

Hello. Jennifer here. It's been awhile.

As I logged on to my blog to write this, I went back and read my last entry—the one I wrote in November. Wow. I knew I wasn't exactly bringing my A-game, but I had no idea how far I'd fallen into unhealthy patterns until I took a good look at the big picture.

The wakeup call was the doctor's visit I had a week after I wrote the last blog back in November. I found a lump. I can honestly say that the days leading up to and following that doctor's visit were the scariest days of my life. The bottom line is that the biopsy revealed a benign (thank God) tumor which was removed in an outpatient procedure.

I guess that could have been the end of the story—I dodged a bullet and that was that. Back to life. But as you might imagine, I did a lot of soul-searching in those days I had off. Nothing brings perspective like a crisis.

I thought back to the days when I started teaching. I was twenty-two years old and right out of college. Everything worked back then. I had energy. I had enthusiasm. I had a sense of purpose and calling when I stepped on to my campus. The drift away from that place was so gradual I never even noticed I was drifting.

When my doctor laid out the health risks I was facing physically due to my lifestyle, I knew something had to change. I've changed my eating habits, and I'm walking four times a week. My weight hasn't changed dramatically, but I have had some compliments, and I'm pretty sure I'm moving in the right direction. I'm still trying to cut back on caffeine, but I'm not going to obsess about it. I'm pleased with the changes I've made so far, and I know that change will continue to happen in due time.

The medical issues also brought more financial stress. Finances are still rough. Gains? Yes. Huge gains? Definitely not. We've consolidated our debt into a low-interest loan, which have made our monthly payment more manageable. We're still developing the self-discipline to track our daily spending and keep on top of things.

Remember Donna? The teacher I had been meaning to ask for help but didn't trust? When she heard about my medical issues, she was so kind to me! She had my students write me get-well cards, and she organized teachers to bring our family meals while I was out. We had a good talk, and I realized how much emotional baggage I was carrying from my last campus that had nothing to do with her or where I am now. I have forgiven my previous administrator, and let me tell you, Donna's kindness to me has been nothing short of healing in my heart. Now, instead of dreading my interaction with her, I actually miss her if we don't have a chance to connect from week to week.

Now that I'm more connected at work, I'm remembering why I went into education. I'm actually feeling excited again about the kids. I've been to a workshop on teaching English Language Learners, and I've found some great resources for classroom management. If I'm honest, I have to say that I still don't know how my kids will do on the test this year. I'm hopeful. Regardless of their performance, though, I can say with honesty now that I will get to the end of the year knowing that I've given it my all.

All in all, I must say that what was a scary and unnerving week back in November ended up being something of a blessing in disguise. Before that week, I was drifting—slowly and without knowing, moving away from the best life I could live. Now, I'm shifting— slowly but this time deliberately moving back to my purpose and calling. It's taking effort, but it sure feels good. As I've started living out my new life, I realize now that it doesn't necessarily take a crisis to motivate someone to change. Change is hard work, but its do-able work.

Well, it's 10:00 p.m. now. Time for bed.

Thanks for reading.

-Jennifer

Conclusion

You went into education to impact students' lives. You weren't wrong. You do have power to make lives better: not only students' lives, but also your own.

I'll conclude by drawing from personal experience to speak to you on behalf of your current Most Likely and the fifty million students enrolled in compulsory education in the United States. Some of those students are obviously needy. Some are quietly desperate. Some are doing just fine. All of them are influenced by the adults in the building.

"Hello sir. Hello ma'am. Thank you for coming to work today.

I don't know where I'll end up when I'm nineteen. I may be earning academic honors at an Ivy League university. I may be serving my country in the military. I may be an employed high school graduate. I may be in jail. I may not even make it to nineteen. Only God knows. Regardless of where I might be and what I might be doing at nineteen, our interaction—you, the teacher and me, the student—shapes me.

You need to know that even though this school building sometimes may seem like a zoo to you, in some very important ways, this school building can be the safest place on earth for me. You need to know that when you are teaching me, even at your worst, you are a better influence on me than much of what (and who) I experience off this campus. And you need to know that when you love me, even at your worst, you love me more sincerely and effectively than many people I'm around away from this campus.

The state gives me tests once a year that measures some of what you've taught me. Life gives me tests every day that measures all of what you've taught me.

So, thank you for teaching me, especially in those moments when every part of my being is communicating that I don't want to be taught by you. And thank you for loving me, especially in those moments when every part of my being is communicating that I don't want to be loved by you.

The bottom line is that I need you. I need to know that you care about me. I need to know that I do not make the rules. And I may never be fortunate enough to appreciate and express that—or even realize that— but I do hope you are courageous enough never to forget it.

Thank you for coming to work today, sir. Thank you for coming to work today, ma'am. Please come back tomorrow."

To you, my teacher friend: Be encouraged. Be enlightened. Be well.

Resource One: Body Mass Index
Courtesy of the American Medical Association
http://www.ama-assn.org/ama1/pub/upload/mm/433/weight.pdf

Figure 2.2 Body Mass Index Chart

Height (inches)	Normal						Overweight					Obese										Extreme obesity														
BMI	19	20	21	22	23	24	25	26	27	28	29	30	31	32	33	34	35	36	37	38	39	40	41	42	43	44	45	46	47	48	49	50	51	52	53	54
												Body weight (pounds)																								
58	91	96	100	105	110	115	119	124	129	134	138	143	148	153	158	162	167	172	177	181	186	191	196	201	205	210	215	220	224	229	234	239	244	248	253	258
59	94	99	104	109	114	119	124	128	133	138	143	148	153	158	163	168	173	178	183	188	193	198	203	208	212	217	222	227	232	237	242	247	252	257	262	267
60	97	102	107	112	118	123	128	133	138	143	148	153	158	163	168	174	179	184	189	194	199	204	209	215	220	225	230	235	240	245	250	255	261	266	271	276
61	100	106	111	116	122	127	132	137	143	148	153	158	164	169	174	180	185	190	195	201	206	211	217	222	227	232	238	243	248	254	259	264	269	275	280	285
62	104	109	115	120	126	131	136	142	147	153	158	164	169	175	180	186	191	196	202	207	213	218	224	229	235	240	246	251	256	262	267	273	278	284	289	295
63	107	113	118	124	130	135	141	146	152	158	163	169	175	180	186	191	197	203	208	214	220	225	231	237	242	248	254	259	265	270	278	282	287	293	299	304
64	110	116	122	128	134	140	145	151	157	163	169	174	180	186	192	197	204	209	215	221	227	232	238	244	250	256	262	267	273	279	285	291	296	302	308	314
65	114	120	126	132	138	144	150	156	162	168	174	180	186	192	198	204	210	216	222	228	234	240	246	252	258	264	270	276	282	288	294	300	306	312	318	324
66	118	124	130	136	142	148	155	161	167	173	179	186	192	198	204	210	216	223	229	235	241	247	253	260	266	272	278	284	291	297	303	309	315	322	328	334
67	121	127	134	140	146	153	159	166	172	178	185	191	198	204	211	217	223	230	236	242	249	255	261	268	274	280	287	293	299	306	312	319	325	331	338	344
68	125	131	138	144	151	158	164	171	177	184	190	197	203	210	216	223	230	236	243	249	256	262	269	276	282	289	295	302	308	315	322	328	335	341	348	354
69	128	135	142	149	155	162	169	176	182	189	196	203	209	216	223	230	236	243	250	257	263	270	277	284	291	297	304	311	318	324	331	338	345	351	358	365
70	132	139	146	153	160	167	174	181	188	195	202	209	216	222	229	236	243	250	257	264	271	278	285	292	299	306	313	320	327	334	341	348	355	362	369	376
71	136	143	150	157	165	172	179	186	193	200	208	215	222	229	236	243	250	257	265	272	279	286	293	301	308	315	322	329	338	343	351	358	365	372	379	386
72	140	147	154	162	169	177	184	191	199	206	213	221	228	235	242	250	258	265	272	279	287	294	302	309	316	324	331	338	346	353	361	368	375	383	390	397
73	144	151	159	166	174	182	189	197	204	212	219	227	235	242	250	257	265	272	280	288	295	302	310	318	325	333	340	348	355	363	371	378	386	393	401	408
74	148	155	163	171	179	186	194	202	210	218	225	233	241	249	256	264	272	280	287	295	303	311	319	326	334	342	350	358	365	373	381	389	396	404	412	420
75	152	160	168	176	184	192	200	208	216	224	232	240	248	256	264	272	279	287	295	303	311	319	327	335	343	351	359	367	375	383	391	399	407	415	423	431
76	156	164	172	180	189	197	205	213	221	230	238	246	254	263	271	279	287	295	304	312	320	328	336	344	353	361	369	377	385	394	402	410	418	426	435	443

References

Achinstein, Betty. *The Ties that Blind: Community, Diversity, and Conflict Among Schoolteachers.* New York, NY: Teachers College Press, 2009.

Alcorn, Randy. *Money, Possessions and Eternity.* Wheaton, IL: Tyndale House Publishers, Inc, 2003.

Allegrante, John., and John Michela. "Impact of school-based workplace health on morale of inner-city teachers." *Journal of School Health, Vol. 60,* (1990): 25-29.

Amschler, Denise, and James McKenzie. "Perceived sleepiness, sleep habits, and sleep concerns of public school teachers, administrators, and other personnel." *American Journal of Health Education,* no.41 (2010): 102-109.

Anderson, Greg. *The 22 Non-negotiable Laws of Wellness: Feel, Think, and Live Better Than You Ever Though Possible.* New York, NY. Harper Collins, 1995.

Anspaugh, David. *Wellness: Concepts and Applications, 4th Ed.* New York, NY: McGraw-Hill, 2000.

Ardell, Donald. *The Book of Wellness: A Secular Approach to Spirituality, Meaning, and Purpose.* Amherst, NY: Prometheus Books,1996.

Arloski, Michael. *Wellness Coaching for Lasting Lifestyle Change.* Duluth, MN: Whole Person Associates, 2009.

Bailey, Kathleen., Allen Curtis, and David Nunan. *Pursuing Professional Development: The Self as Source.* Boston, MA: Heinle and Heinle, 2001.

Baumeister, Roy and others. *Then a Miracle Occurs: Focusing on Behavior in Social Psychological Theory and Research.* New York, NY: Oxford University Press, 2005.

Bender, William and Cara Shores. *Response to Intervention: A Practical Guide for Every Teacher.* Thousand Oaks, CA: Corwin Press, Inc, 2007.

Benson, Herbert. *The Wellness Book: The Comprehensive Guide to Maintaining Health and Treating Stress-Related Illness.* New York, NY: Scribner, 1992.

Brenner, Stenlof. "The stress chain: a longitudinal confirmatory study of teacher stress, coping, and social support." *Journal of Occupational Psychology, Vol. 58*, (1985):1-13.

Brophy, Jere and Thomas Good. *Teacher behavior and student achievement. In M.C.*

Wittrock (Ed.), Handbook of research on teaching, 3rd Ed. New York, NY: Macmillan, 1986.

Bulger, Sean. (2002). "Stack the deck in favor of your students by using the four aces of teaching." *Journal of Effective Teaching* 5, no. 2 (2002).

Burden, Paul. *Classroom Management: Creating a Successful K-12 Learning   Community, Third Edition.* Hoboken, NJ: John Wiley & Sons, Inc, 2006.

Bryk, Anthony and Barbara Schneider. *Trust in Schools: A core resource for improvement.* Chicago, IL: Russell Sage Foundation, 2002.

Covey, Steven. *The Seven Habits of Highly Effective People.* New York, NY: Simon and Schuster, Inc, 1989.

Cleary, Thomas. *I Ching: The Book of Change.* Boston, MA: Shambhala Publications, Inc, 1992.

Clinton, Tim and Gary Sibcy. *Attachments: Why You Love, Feel and Act the Way You Do.* Brentwood, TN: Integrity Publishers, 2002.

Colbert, Don. *Stress Management 101.* Nashville, TN: Thomas Nelson, Inc, 2006.

Connors, Neila. *If You Don't Feed the Teachers, They Eat the Students: Guide to Success for Administrators and Teachers.* Nashville, TN: Incentive Publications, 2000.

Csikszentmihalyi, Mihali. *Flow.* New York, NY: Harper Collins Publishers, 1990.

Davis, Martha and Eshelman Robbins. *The Relaxation and Stress Reduction Workbook.* New York, NY: New Harbinger Publications, Inc, 1995.

Davis, Lynn, Karina Loyo, and others. "A comprehensive worksite wellness program in Austin, Texas: Partnership between steps to a healthier Austin and capital Metropolitan transportation authority.*"* *Preventing Chronic Disease 6*, no. 2 (2009).

deSouza, Junior. *Be Yourself: Finding and Freeing Your Truest Self Biblically.* Longwood, FL: Xulon Press, 2007.

Dinham, Stephen, and Corbin Scott. "An international comparative study of teacher satisfaction, motivation, and health: Australia, England, and New Zealand." *Paper Presented at the Annual Meeting of the American Educational Research Association; April 13-17; San Diego, CA, (*1998*).*

Durka, Glora. *The Teacher's Calling: A Spirituality for Those Who Teach.* Muhwah, NJ: Paulist Press, 2002.

Dodge, Judith. *Differentiation in Action.* New York, NY: Scholastic Inc, 2005.

Elliot, Charles and Laura Smith. *Overcoming Anxiety for Dummies.* New York, NY:

Wiley Publishing Inc, 2003 .

Erickson, Jill and Catherine Gillespie. "Reasons women discontinued participation in an exercise and wellness program." *The Physical Educator vol. 51,* no.1 (2000): 2-7.

Flippen, Flip and Christopher White. *The Flip Side: Break Free of the Behaviors That Hold You Back.* New York, NY: SpringBoard Press, 2007.

Forsten, Char, John Grant, and Becki Hollas. *Differentiated Instruction: Different Strategies for Different Learners.* Petersborough, NH: Crystal Springs Books, 2002.

Gilbert, Roberta. *Extraordinary Relationships: A New Way of Thinking About Human Interactions.* New York, NY: John Wiley & Sons, Inc, 1992.

Glatthorn, Allen, Floyd Boschee and Bruce Whitehead. *Curriculum Leadership: Development and Implementation.* Thousand Oaks, CA: Sage Publications Inc, 2006.

Goddard, Yvonne and Megan Tschannen-Moran. "A theoretical and empirical investigation of teacher collaboration for school improvement and student achievement in public elementary schools." *Teachers College Record 109* no. 4 (2007): 877-896.

Gordon, Jon. *Energy Addict: 101 Physical, Occupational, and Spiritual Ways to Energize Your Life.* New York, NY: Perigee, The Berkley Publishing Group, 2003.

Gottman, Jon. *Raising an Emotionally Intelligent Child.* New York, NY: Fireside, 1997.

Gregory, Gayle and Carlyn Chapman. *Differentiated Instructional Strategies: One Size Doesn't Fit All.* Thousand Oaks, CA: Corwin Press, Inc, 2002.

Guarino, Cassandra, Lucrecia Santibanez and Glen Daley. "Teacher recruitment and retention: A review of the recent empirical literature." *Review of Educational Research 76,* no. 2 (2006): 173-208.

Hartney, Elizabeth. *Stress Management for Teachers.* New York, NY: Continuum International Publishing Group, 2008.

Henderson, Nan and Mike Milstein. *Resiliency in Schools: Making It Happen for Students and Educators.* Thousand Oaks, CA: Corwin Press, Inc, 2003.

Herman Rebecca and others. "Turning around chronically low-performing schools: A practiceguide (NCEE #2008-4020)." *U.S. Department of Education, Institute of Education Sciences, National Center for Education Evaluation and Regional Assistance,* (2008).

Hess, F.M., and M.J. Petrilli. *No Child Left Behind.* New York, NY: Peter Lang   Publishing, Inc, 2006.

Hoffman, B., and J. Deitch. *Discover Wellness.* Eagan, MN: Center Path Publishing,2007.

Hyman, M. *Ultra-Metabolism: The Simple Plan for Automatic Weight Loss.* New York, NY: Scribner, 2006.

ING. "A Lesson Learned: ING Survey Finds Teachers Have a Profound and Lasting Impact On Our Lives, Yet Are Vastly Underappreciated." ING,

http://ing.us/about-ing/newsroom/press-releases/lesson-learned-ing-survey-finds-teachers-have-profound-and-lasting.

Jampolsky, Gerald and J. Denver. *Goodbye To Guilt: Releasing Fear Through Forgiveness.* New York, NY: Bantam Books, 1985.

Jimerson, Shane and Matthew Burns. *Handbook of Response to Intervention: The Science and Practice of Assessment and Intervention.* New York, NY: Springer Science Business Media, LLC, 2007.

Kardos, Susan and Susan Johnson. (2007). "On their own and presumed expert: New teachers' experience with their colleagues." *Teachers College Record vol.109,* no. 9 (2007): 2083-2106.

Karen, Robert. *Becoming Attached: First Relationships and How They Shape Our Capacity to Love.* New York, NY: Oxford University Press, 1998.

Kemerer, Frank and Jim Walsh. *The Educator's Guide to Texas School Law, 4th Edition.* Austin, TX: University of Texas Press, 1996.

Klusmann, Uta and Jurgen Trautwein. (2008). "Teachers' occupational wellbeing quality of instruction: the role of self-regulatory patterns." *Journal of Educational Psychology, Vol. 100,* no 3(2008).

Kochanek, Julie. *Building Trust for Better Schools.* Corwin Press: Thousand Oaks, CA, 2005.

Krassnoer, Paul. *An impolite interview with Paul Krassner (The Realist).* New York, NY: Seven Stories Press, 1963.

Levinson, Robert and Charles Aldwin. "Positive emotional change: mediating effects of forgiveness and spirituality." *The Journal of Science and Healing, Vol. 2,* no. 6 (2006): 498-508.

MacCaskey, Michael and Bill Marken, and National Gardening Association. *Gardening for Dummies, Second Edition.* New York, NY: Wiley Publishing, Inc, 1999.

Martin, James. *Becoming Who You Are.* Mahwah, NJ: HiddenSpring, 2006.

Maslach, Christina. *Burnout: The Cost of Caring.* Cambridge, MA: Malor Books, 2003.

Maslach, Christina and Michael Leiter. *The Truth About Burnout.* New York, NY: John Wiley & Sons, Inc, 1997.

May, Rollo. *The Meaning of Anxiety.* New York, NY: The Ronald Press Company, 1977.

McCullough, Michael, Giacomo Bono, and Lindsey Root. (2007). "Rumination, emotion, and forgiveness: three longitudinal studies." *Journal of Personality and Social Psychology, Vol. 92,* no. 3 (2007): 490-505.

Mellard, Daryl and Evelyn Johnson. *RTI: A Practitioner's Guide to Implementing Response toIntervention.* Thousand Oaks, CA: Corwin Press Inc., 2008.

Minow, Martha. *Between Vengeance and Forgiveness: Facing History After Genocide and Mass Violence.* Boston, MA: Beacon Press, 1998.

Nieto, Sonya. *What Keeps Teachers Going?* New York, NY: Teachers College Press, 2003.

Orman, Suze. *Nine Steps to Financial Freedom.* New York: Three Rivers Press, 2001.

Palmer, Parker. *To Know as We Are Known.* Harper Collins: New York, 1983.

Palmer, Parker. *Let Your Life Speak: Listening for the Voice of Vocation.* San Francisco, CA: Jossey Bass, 2000.

Palmer, Parker. *The courage to teach: Exploring the inner landscape of a teacher's life.* San Fransisco: Jossey-Bass, 2007.

Peck, Scott. *The Road Less Traveled: A New Psychology of Love, Traditional Values and Spiritual Growth.* New York, NY: Simon and Schuster, 1978.

Pink, Dan. *Drive: The Surprising Truth About What Motivates Us.* New York, NY: Penguin Group, 2009.

Phillips, Samantha, Dil Sen, and Roseanne McNamee."Risk factors for work-related stress andhealth in head teachers." *Occupational Medicine; Vol.58,* no.8 (2008): 584-586.

Queen, Allen and Patsy Queen. *The Frazzled Teacher's Wellness Plan: A Five Step Program for Reclaiming Time, Managing Stress, and Creating a Healthy Lifestyle.* Thousand Oaks, CA: Corwin Press, 2004.

Ramsey, Dave. *Financial Peace Revisited.* Nashville, TN: Thomas Nelson, 2003.

Ramsey, Dave. *The Total Money Makeover: A Proven Plan for Financial Fitness.* Nashville, TN: Thomas Nelson, 2009.

Rath, Tom and J. Harter. *Wellbeing: The Five Essential Elements.* New York, NY: Gallup   Press, 2010.

Resnicon, Kelly and others. "Results of the TeachWell worksite wellness program." *American Journal of Public Health, Vol. 88,* no. 2 (1998): 250-257.

Richo, David. *How To Be An Adult: A Handbook on Psychological and Spiritual Integration.* Muhwah, NJ: Paulist Press, 1991.

Richo, David. *How to be an Adult in Relationships: The Five Keys to Mindful Loving.* Boston, MA: Shambhala Publications, Inc, 2002.

Rosenshine, Barak and Nelly Furst. *Research on teacher performance criteria. In B. O. Smith (Ed.), Research in teacher education: A symposium.* Englewood Cliffs, NH: Prentice-Hall, 1973.

Rubleski, Jeff. *10 essential steps to financial wellness.* Omaha, NE: Wellness Counsels of America, 2006.

Sadleir, Steve. *Looking for God: A Seeker's Guide to Religious and Spiritual Groups of the World.* New York, NY: The Berkley Publishing Group, 2000.

Sears, Barry and Bill Lawren. *The Zone: A Dietary Road Map.* New York, NY: HarperCollins Publishers, Inc, 1995.

Shelton, Carla and Alice Pollingue. *The Exceptional Teacher's Handbook: The First-Year Special Education Teacher's Guide for Success.* Thousand Oaks, CA:

Corwin Press, Inc., 2001

Smith, Huston. *The World's Religions.* New York, NY: HarperCollins Publishers Inc, 1991.

Smith, Thomas and Richard Ingersoll. "What are the Effects of Induction and Mentoring on Beginning Teacher Turnover?" *American Educational Research Journal Vol. 41*, no. 3 (2004): 681-714.

Stanley, Thomas and William Danko. *The Millionaire Next Door: The Surprising Secrets of America's Wealthy.* New York, NY: Pocket Books, 1996.

Stephens, Ronald *Safe Schools: A Handbook for Violence Prevention.* Bloomington, IN: National Education Service, 1995.

Stephens, Ronald and June Arnette. *Policy and Procedure Guide for Creating Safe Schools.* Malibu, CA: National School Safety Center, 1994.

Tillich, Paul. *The Courage to Be.* New Haven, CT: Yale University Press, 1952.

Toussaint, Loren and Jon Webb. (2010). *Theoretical and Empirical Connections Between Forgiveness, Mental Health, and Well-Being, In E. L. Worthington (Ed.), Handbook of Forgiveness.* New York, NY: Brunner-Routledge, 2010.

Travis, John and Regina Ryan. *The Wellness Workbook.* Celestial Arts: Berkeley, CA, 2004.

Umbarger, Carter. *Structural Family Therapy.* New York, NY: Grune and Stratton, Inc, 1983.

Walls, Richard. *Concepts of learning: 99 truths. In Federal Emergency Management Agency (Ed.), Instructor one.* Emmitsburg, MD: National Emergency Training Center, 1994.

Whitaker, Todd. *Dealing with Difficult Teachers 2nd Edition.* Larchmont, NY: Eye On Education, Inc., 2002.

Whitaker, Todd, and D. Fiore. *Dealing with Difficult Parents: And with Parents in Difficult Situations.* Larchmont, NY: Eye On Education, Inc, 2001.

Whitaker, Todd, and J. Winkle. *Feeling Great! The Educator's Guide for Eating Better, Exercising Smarter, and Feeling Your Best.* Larchmont, NY: Eye On Education, 2002.

Willerman, Lee and Dennis Cohen. *Psychopathology.* New York, NY: McGraw-Hill, Inc, 1990.

Winnicott, David. *Playing and Reality.* London, England: Tavistock Publications Ltd, 1971.

Worthington, El and others. "Forgiveness in health research and medical practice." *The Journal of Science and Healing, Vol. 1,* no. 3 (2005): 169-176.

Wright, Paul. *Wrightslaw: Special Education Law 2nd Edition.* Hartfield, VI: Harbor House Law Press, Inc, 2007.

Wright, Paul and Steve. Heath. *No Child Left Behind.* Hartfield, VI: Harbor House Law Press, Inc., 2004.

XuShaungshuang, PengDanpin, and WeiYan. "The Study on Occupational Wellbeing of the Primary School Teachers." *Global Journal of Human Social Science.* Volume 11, no. 9 (2011).

Young, Jeff, Janet Klosko, and Aaron Beck. *Reinventing Your Life.* New York, NY: Plume, 1994.

To book Adam L. Sáenz for a keynote or
workshop at your school or event,
please use the contact information below:

Adam L. Sáenz, Ph.D., D.Min.
2554 East Villa Maria
Bryan, Texas 77802
Phone: 979-229-7636
Fax: 979-774-016
Email: adam@adamsaenz.com
www.thepowerofateacher.com

Intermedia Publishing Group

Publishing That Works For You

Whether you want to purchase bulk copies of *The Power of a Teacher* or buy another book for a friend,
get it now at:
www.imprbooks.com.

If you have a book that you would like to publish,
contact Terry Whalin, Publisher, at Intermedia Publishing
Group, (623) 337-8710 or
email: **twhalin@intermediapub.com**
or use the contact form at: **www.intermediapub.com**.